composition

contrast

complexity

composition

Francine Houben

contrast

Mecanoo Architects

complexity

Photography: Christian Richters

Birkhäuser - Publishers for Architecture
Basel · Boston · Berlin

Contents

Introduction 7
Ten statements 9
Intermezzo 1 – Urban renewal 28
Intermezzo 2 – Memories of Gerrit Rietveld 33
Amsterdam canals – Canal house and L.A. Rieshuis, Amsterdam 37
Twelve houses and a hotel – House and studio, Rotterdam 43
Dancing blocks – Ringvaartplasbuurt Oost, Prinsenland, Rotterdam 51
Space for space – Reorganisation of public space, Groningen city centre 63
Intimacy and reconciliation – Herdenkingsplein [Commemorative Square], Maastricht . 71
Kasbah in the polder – Faculty of Economics and Management, Utrecht 79
School of the senses – Isala College, Silvolde 91
Church and theatre – Trusttheater, Amsterdam 103
The ruin of beauty – Castle Ruins Cultural Centre, Deurne 115
Library of the future – Library, Delft Technical University 123
Changement – Westergasfabriek, Amsterdam 135
Eco town, nature town, water town – Almere 2015 143
Gesture in the landscape – National Heritage Museum, Arnhem 151
A house to work in – Maliebaan 16, Utrecht 163
Triumph of Spirit over Matter – Opera décor 175
St Mary of the Angels – R.C. Chapel, Rotterdam 183
Between the Rotte and the motorway – Nieuw Terbregge, Rotterdam 191
Rhapsody in Blue – Parkhotel, Rotterdam 203
Mecanoo Blue – 4th Bienal Internacional de Arquitetura, São Paulo 211
A room with a view – Art of engineering and aesthetics of mobility 219

Project specifications 233
Biography Francine Houben 237
Bibliography 239
Selected awards 251
Selected exhibitions 251
Mecanoo 2001 253

Introduction

This book is about my experiences. I present how I see things, my opinions and my feelings about architecture. I have made a selection from the many Mecanoo projects. A house and a canalside residence. A garden city and a city of water. A secondary school, a polytechnic and a university library. The public space of a historic city, a park and a square in a medieval city. A vision of mobility and infrastructure and an ecological new town. A hotel and an underground office. A ruin, a theatre, a décor for an opera, a museum and an exhibition. And finally a chapel in a cemetery. Each of them is a project in which I have been able to flex my conceptual muscles. They are typical of how I see things and illustrate the three core concepts in my view of architecture: composition, contrast and complexity.

I learned to analyse, to think in scale levels, and to deal with the complexity of architectural assignments as an architecture student at Delft Technical University. The practical classes by Max Risselada played an important role in this. He emphasised the need not to fall back on simple one-liners and showed me the art with which you can interweave urban planning, architectural and technical aspects in a single solution. He used exhibitions to show the difference in their approach to space between Adolf Loos and Le Corbusier. Together with Erick van Egeraat I discovered the work of Charles and Ray Eames, for which I have developed a fond attachment, like that of Alison and Peter Smithson. We travelled a lot and met other architects. We wanted to see and experience architecture all over the world.

Ray Eames gave me a sense of composition. The visits I have made to her home and to her office since 1978 have made a lasting impression on me. She had mastered the art of arrangement, of putting together what you collect, what you come across. She and Charles designed houses, chairs and exhibitions that are still beautiful fifty years later. For me this is evidence that there are lasting values in architecture and design that are based on beauty appreciated by the senses. After all, beauty is about primal emotions.

Mecanoo has taught me the fun of working together, the feeling that you are sharing something special. Over the years Mecanoo has changed from a firm of architects for housing to a firm of architects for architecture, urban planning, landscape and infrastructure. With more than fifty members of staff, Mecanoo has grown to become a firm with an international reputation. It is a privilege to direct the design processes together with Henk Döll in the professional working atmosphere of the bureau. This is the climate where concepts take root, and arrive at their final form after a lot of argument and agreement. I am especially grateful in this respect to the designers and engineers Michel Tombal, Aart Fransen, Iemke Bakker, Sjaak Janssen, Sylvie Beugels, Annelies van Eenennaam, Leen Kooman, Ana Rocha, Berthe Jongejan, Joke Klumper, Francesco Veenstra, Carlo Bevers, Alfa Hügelmann, Anthony Hoete, Huib de Jong, Toon de Wilde, Anne Busker, and Ellen van der Wal. And to Henk Bouwer for making the scale models. Moreover, there is a whole new generation of designers and engineers in the bureau who are already making an important contribution. We design together from detail to infrastructure, and we confuse the distinction between landscape and architecture. In this context we create the space for attractive, idiosyncratic architecture.

Hans Andersson encouraged me to write this book. It is the story as I tell it in my lectures: personal and inspired. Hanneke Hollander has supported me with endless patience and carried out the final editing.

The special advisers with whom I have worked are the source of my ideas about an integrated art of engineering. Interesting developments in architecture spring from those who manage to create the freedom within the fragmented practice of design and architecture to experiment and to work together. I would like to single out Arie Krijgsman and Walter Spangenberg of ABT engineering consultancy for special mention. They were, with their bureau, responsible for the construction of many of the projects described here.

Architects nowadays are not asked to come up with a simple design for a building or a block of houses. There is a plurality of design assignments: a vision for the future with sustainable values, the relation to the city and the landscape, the integration of the unpredictable, the mood and application of the use of materials, the importance of mobility, and helping to solve political and social problems. The architectural assignment today covers not only the individual building, irrespective of how idiosyncratic, big and dominant it may be, but also the treacherous anonymity of housing, the scale and identity of the city, and the future of the changing landscape.

In the last resort, architecture cannot be formulated in words. The twenty projects tell a story. The ten statements summarise the views on which they are based. Or rather: they make it clear what I am looking for.

Francine Houben

1.

Land as an expensive commodity
The difference between Los Angeles and Tokyo is obvious to everyone. Los Angeles, the city of the twentieth century, designed for the car which is literally given more room than people are: there are more square metres of car parks than of built-up areas. There is an abundance of land and it is almost valueless. This is bound to change in the twenty-first century.

Tokyo, the gigantic village of millions of people and public transport. Every square metre has been thought about and put to use, above ground and below it. Land is very expensive, even more expensive than the houses and buildings that stand on it.

The Netherlands, a country with a high population density and a shortage of land. At the same time the country that wastes its land because the price of land is much too low. The result is a lack of intelligent solutions such as dual use of land, inventive combinations of infrastructure and building.

2.

Love of nature
The Netherlands, the most malleable country in the world. The land of water, wind and clouds. The Dutch landscape is not static, but it is changeable with contrasting ingredients: order and chaos, polders and lakes, canals and wetlands, dykes and river forelands, wet and dry. With the help of engineers you can build everywhere. There are no limits, the land is so malleable that you can destroy it too.

Nature has an irreplaceable value and beauty, many colours, materials and textures. I want to draw on the wealth of water, skies, trees and leaves, grass, stones and rocks. I use materials like wood, bamboo, zinc, copper, concrete, glass and steel in compositions full of contrasts.

3.

Collective responsibility for sustainability
The Netherlands is a country with a very strong tradition in the field of collective responsibility for the management of the water. Unambiguous agreements regulate the land and the water – literally, because otherwise we would all drown. The collective responsibility for water management should be extended to a collective responsibility for the sustainability of how the country is ordered. After all, that too is a question of the survival of us all.

4.

Wealth of urban planning
It is as if we have forgotten the wealth of urban planning possibilities for housing. The house with a garden and a car in front seems to be the greatest good on earth at the moment. Society consists of very diverse types of family and an ageing population, and it is multicultural. The steadily expanding potential of technology, communication and services will become part of new ideas about housing and care and homes for work and recreation too. The acquisition of mobility, the car, calls for integration in new urban planning typologies without dominating or disrupting the public space. We must design buildings and houses that, like the time-hallowed Dutch villas, can stand up to the big changes in time, use and beauty.

5.

Cooperation as challenge
Interesting developments in architecture are produced by those who manage to create the freedom to experiment and to work together within the fragmented practice of design and building. As a result of changes in the design assignments, architects increasingly carry out their profession in collaboration with other disciplines. In order to achieve the aesthetic of mobility, I want to work with road and hydraulic engineers and landscape architects. This means experimenting with combined programmes, constructions, water and materials, but emphatically without the loss of the architect's own role and responsibility.

6.

Director and script writer
The Van Nelle factory, the Rietveld Schröder house and Amsterdam-Zuid by Berlage are traditional examples of innovative architecture resulting from an inspiring relation between client and architect. Times have changed and the placing of commissions has become more diffuse, consisting of forms of association between the government, property developers, investors and consumers. The architect no longer supplies the design alone. The architect performs the role of director and script writer in a more hybrid process. The architect tries to find out what the client really wants by means of ideas, images, atmospheres, scale models and drawings.

7.

Handwriting and language

Discussion about style is interesting, but not essential in the long run. The best example of this is the composition of two houses that we developed for Alvaro Siza in The Hague: one in the style of the Amsterdam School, the other in the style of Neue Sachlichkeit – two styles that competed with one another in the Twenties and each thought it was the true one. The beauty of the project lies in the combination of introverted and extroverted, heavy and light, tactile and abstract. Style is an outdated phenomenon. Architecture needs a handwriting that can write in different languages in order to be able to respond adequately to each location and assignment.

8.

Composition of empty space
There are no rules for making a composition. The most I can do is to refer to a Japanese book describing the rules for arranging and serving a meal. Working with unambiguous geometry and symmetry is strictly prohibited because it is not exciting. Space, or rather empty space, is an essential part of composition, rhythm and elegance. The space between contrasting forms, round and square, long and short, big and small, brings out each form better, and this is true in architecture as well.

9.

Analysis and intuition
You can try to analyse everything, but a lot is just a question of intuition. The work of David Hockney has always appealed to me. I detect a non-dogmatic, optimistic attitude to life in his work, and the courage to experiment in art with new techniques. An attitude like that is a source of energy and resilience within the complex force field of architectural practice. And the combination of analysis with intuition is worth its weight in gold for architecture.

10.

Arrangement of form and emotion
Charles and Ray Eames were able to combine technical, human and playful aspects in a single solution. They experimented with new materials for their chairs and discovered their limitations as they went along. That led them to look for new solutions all over again. They were designers without dogmatism, and never lost sight of comfort. They are the uncrowned king and queen of arrangement. Their work has a permanent inspiring value. Their house was built in 1949 in the hills of Santa Monica near Los Angeles, in a beautiful setting behind the eucalyptus trees.
It shows what happens when you combine the technical with the sensorial. Architecture must appeal to all the senses and is never a purely intellectual, conceptual or visual game alone. Architecture is about combining all of the individual elements in a single concept. What counts in the last resort is the arrangement of form and emotion.

Youth housing project, Kruisplein, Rotterdam

UNESCO competition Tomorrow's Habitat

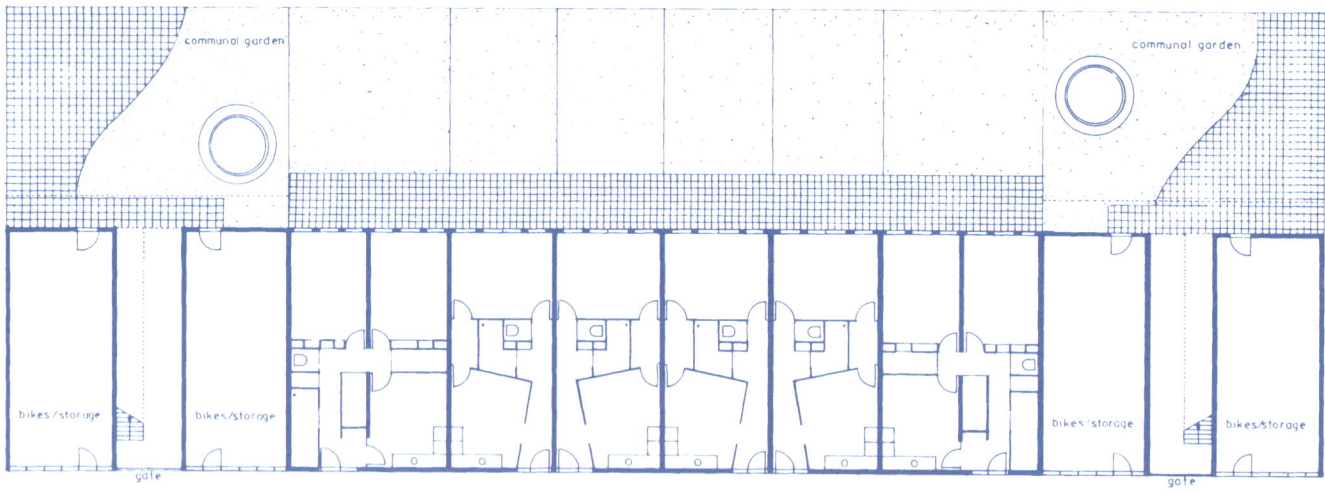

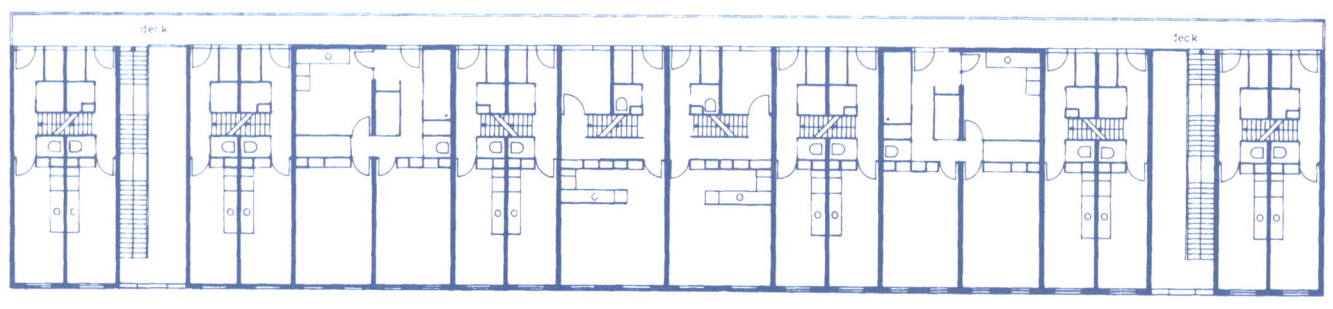

Kruisplein youth housing

In 1980 we win the competition for youth housing in the Kruisplein in Rotterdam. We want to show that a high architectural quality is possible within the practice of urban renewal and housing policy. Council housing can – no, must – be attractive too. The city and its residents must be able to be proud of it. We spend ages on working out the ground plan. These are not houses for the average family, but multi-functional units for a large group of people who no longer live in a family setting. The whole spatial organisation of the building is put together as a housing machine. At the same time we include fitting into the existing surrounding, the treatment of the outer wall, the careful selection of materials, the technical details, the lighting and the colour scheme. We want to do everything. We even choose the tree in the square – a tree of heaven – ourselves. The client has confidence in the plan and follows us. Later on we discover that a special relation with the client is a condition for carrying out path-breaking concepts.

UNESCO

Before the Kruisplein project is completed in 1985, I want to show that the renewal of council housing can be done not only in an unusual location with a unique programme, but also in ordinary streets in neighbourhoods in the nineteenth-century ring of Dutch cities. The – open – submission to the interna-

Urban renewal

tional UNESCO competition *Tomorrow's Habitat* is about living in the year 2000. The renewal of the city will still be the task then, I am convinced. The winning entry becomes a statement about the future council housing task, the changing composition of the population, and how to deal with it architecturally.

Boy's dream

Winning the Kruisplein and the UNESCO competitions causes a flood of commissions in urban renewal. The Kruisplein project symbolises a change in the practice of council housing and urban renewal. It is not just a plan on paper, but it is carried out while we are still students. It is described in the newspapers as a boy's dream. Apparently girls don't have them, at any rate not in architecture until then. Actually, the real reason for taking part in the international UNESCO competition is because I want to go to Japan. The winner is offered a trip to Japan. The entry wins the first prize in the Netherlands but not internationally, so there is no trip to Japan. But I use the result to apply for a travel grant to go on a much longer journey through Japan – a trip that is to have a major influence on our future work.

Public space

Filling in the seven empty spaces in the street walls of the Bospolder Tussendijken district in Rotterdam is mainly about housing typology and access, and fitting into old neighbourhoods architecturally. The gaps are carefully filled with a housing typology that is based on multiple use and the pride of every resident at having their own front door opening onto the street. The typically Dutch cycle sheds receive special attention. The UNESCO plan is the precursor of these ideas.
We take over the public domain – the public space – with the Tiendplein project in Rotterdam. It includes designing squares, raised decks on top of covered car parks. The city must be given back to the children. Haven't the cars taken over their room for playing in the last few decades? Everyone should be able to

Housing in Hillekop, Rotterdam

live in the city with an attractive public space. After a tough fight with the local authority designers, we eventually design the Zijdewindeplein ourselves: the paving, the benches, the litter bins and the lighting. This square goes with chestnut trees. We poke two big sycamores through the raised deck that bring air and light into the car park and soften the concrete surface of the deck. The deck is a fantastic shelter and a safe place for small children. We even think up the jeu de boules area and a ping-pong table for the residents.

Docklands

The Hillekop project regains the Rijnhaven in Rotterdam as a housing location. The negative stigma of high-rise flats is removed by the comfort of a flat on one floor with a balcony, a lift and above all a wonderful view of the fascinating docklands and river. No corridors like in the Sixties, no monotony or lack of identity, but a tower block with a panoramic view and a compact, sheltered hall, inspired by Alvar Aalto's Neue Vahr housing project in Bremen.

It is only many years later that I see Neue Vahr in real life. To be honest, I think the Hillekop looks much better in its location. I am opposed to the idea that good architecture is about applying original shapes. A shape is not someone's personal property. It is about treating the architecture of the past in a respectful and intelligent way and then going on to formulate an answer in a completely new way to today's design assignment, which is often highly complex and multi-layered. This answer does not just lie in the shape.

Look alikes

Our urban renewal projects are often copied by other architects. You see look alikes springing up in the city. It creates mixed feelings. On the one hand, you are proud and you tell yourself that this was always the intention. You think it up and you want to set an example that has to be copied, because you don't want to repeat those inventions yourself. You want to move on to other challenges. But perhaps you want a sign, a thank you, recognition. I remember a discussion with Ray Eames in 1981. I asked her how she felt about all the chairs designed by her and Charles being copied on a large scale, and often badly. Ray said: 'I don't mind the copying, that's OK. As long as the copies are better.' I have never forgotten that reply.

Gerrit Rietveld died in 1964. I was nine years old at the time. I never met him. I was confronted with his work at four moments in my life.

It is 1960. My parents build a house in the Zandweg in Heerlen. I walk over the site with my father. The latest type of Bruynzeel kitchen is installed in this house. Our kitchen is in bold colours: red, yellow, blue, black and teak. If I think about this house where I lived until I was eight, I see this kitchen. It was designed by a team from Bruynzeel itself. I am convinced that the work and way of thinking of Rietveld influenced this kitchen. It is an industrially manufactured, mass-produced product. That is why the corners have to be right angles. It radiates the optimism and belief in serial mass production.

The Zandweg is long, especially when you are only four years old. The Zandweg is not only long, it is also hilly. I never particularly noticed Van der Slobbe's house at the other end of the Zandweg. It was designed by Rietveld and was built in the same period as my parents' house. We moved home when I was eight. I visit this Rietveld house twenty years later.

It is 1974. My youngest brother makes a table of crates for me. I go to Delft to study architecture. In a student flat. He makes the table as Rietveld had described it in 1935 – pinewood planks 14.5 cm

Memories of Gerrit Rietveld

wide, fastened together with brass screws. Apparently he finds the table too sober for his sister, so he paints it red, white and black as a surprise. The table stands in my student flat in Delft. People often comment on it: the table made of crates should not be painted, that is not original. I was naïve and did not understand. The crate table was once designed by Rietveld so that you could make it yourself, but why shouldn't you be allowed to paint it afterwards? And anyway, it looked terrific! In retrospect it makes me smile. Perhaps that is the deep-seated reason why I am not interested in discussions of style. Perhaps also because I often don't understand critics, especially if they have studied architecture.

It is 1976. I have been studying architecture for two years and I go with a couple of other students on an excursion to the Rietveld Schröder house. Mrs Schröder receives us. We have brought a big cake with us. We sit at the famous table and eat it with her. We sit on the zigzag chairs and Mrs Schröder opens the diagonal window for us. It is cosy and informal. Mrs Schröder fascinates me. She talks lovingly about the house and especially about all the practical and clever devices that she thought up with Rietveld, about planks and slats which all have a specific purpose. Not only we, but she too enjoys us sitting together there. She shows us how tidily she lives. Actually, it is more like a small flat, with a usable floor area of around 100 m². The lower floor is rented to tenants. In fact it is more like a piece of furniture, compact and adaptable. At the same time, you have to organise your things with an iron discipline, just like in a holiday home. That means tidying up all the time and making agreements with one another if you live here with more than one person. And then to think that she lived here with three children.

Mrs Schröder talks about her house as a designed, personal attitude to life. What attracted her about Rietveld was that he lived through his senses, he was not interested in abstraction. The only thing you can be sure of is what you perceive and work on with your senses.

That is your reality. This was important to Mrs Schröder and it is what appealed to her in the work of Rietveld. She found this a safe guide. What she said made an impression on me.

It is 1987. Mrs Schröder is dead. The Rietveld Schröder house has been restored and turned into a museum. I am asked to visit the house with a journalist and to state my impressions. It is strange. In fact, this visit takes away my good memories of the house. It is not a house any longer, but a museum. Everything is pure and above all as it originally was again. The moment I get over the fact that the house has become a museum, I see with new eyes. For instance, I enjoy looking at a lamp, a bulb hanging from a wire with a sheet of glass above it. A wonderful counterblast to all notions of design.

It is 1995. Ida van Zijl from the Centraal Museum invites me to give the Rietveld lecture and I revisit the house. In fact, I see it with new eyes again. In the meantime we have completed a great many projects ourselves. Our finest projects are those which have been carried out in special collaboration with the client. By now I know that there are people who can play the role of an inspiring client.
Now I look with the eyes of an architect. How you make something. I can smile at certain solutions in the house, because of details that you also have to tussle with as an architect. Things have been constantly added to the house because of the specific wishes of its occupant. I like it. Everything has been solved as a carpenter would do it with pine, screws, hinges and a coat of paint on top.

Ida van Zijl asks me what association I have with Rietveld. I reply: 'Not with the Rietveld Schröder house, but the photo from 1918 of Rietveld sitting in front of his furniture workshop in the Adriaen van Ostadelaan in Utrecht, together with his assistants. I can gaze at that photo for a long time. It says something about the period, the man and his assistants. To me he radiates the pride of a craftsman. The pleasure of working together, the feeling that you are doing something special together. That's how I like to feel about my work too.'

The structure of the inner city of Amsterdam was largely determined in the seventeenth century. The combination of the plots of land that are so typical of Holland with the narrow, deep houses and with a façade of classicistic elements from Italy arose in that Golden Age. The merchants of the day wanted the impossible: a house like a palace on a plot of land five or seven-and-a-half metres wide. The town mansions have supporting walls. The façade does not have a constructive function and can be elaborated irrespective of the ground plan behind it. The façade was more or less decorated depending on the available budget of the merchant. That is how the image of the Amsterdam canals was created: unity in diversity. Even façades from later centuries were effortlessly incorporated into the rhythm.

Older homosexuals

Among the houses beside the Brouwersgracht are two houses in deplorable condition. They are not attractive and they do not have the status of historic monuments. Behind them and to one side, in the Vinkenstraat, is a house where everything has been demolished except the ground floor because of fire or problems with the foundations. Both locations are part of a large closed block of buildings, including the old people's home De Rietvinck that was built in the Seventies. Han Michel from De Principaal Housing Association asks us to make a

Amsterdam canals

37
Canal house and
L.A. Rieshuis, Amsterdam

design for both locations, the expensive and the inexpensive one. The inexpensive location in the Vinkenstraat becomes an annex of the old people's home which wants to provide accommodation for the first commune of elderly homosexuals in the Netherlands. Apartments and a studio are planned for the Brouwersgracht location.

On the run

The biggest challenge of the two assignments is how to adapt the design aesthetically to the historic structure of the city. By playing with the materials as well as with the requirements of the Housing Commission, we have designed two subtle complexes with a character entirely of their own. The eleven-metre-wide façade of the Brouwersgracht is divided into a tall, narrow section and a low, wide one. The left-hand half consists of large sliding windows and wooden panels in the brick frame of a façade that tilts slightly forwards. The right-hand half has a calmer division of the window, contained in masonry turned on its side. The details make it a magnificent, light and refined façade. Why Amsterdam façades sometimes tilt slightly forwards as if they are on the run is a matter for controversy among historians. Some say that it stops the water from remaining in the frames so that the wood does not rot so quickly, others suggest that it is connected with the perspective of the façades and the street. Behind these façades are a studio, six city apartments, and a penthouse. The apartments in the right-hand part are narrow with windows around them from the canal to the alley, while those in the left-hand part are wide and face the canal. The kitchen and bathroom have been positioned to ensure a maximum of free space: a loft. The façade in the alley tilts slightly backwards and thereby meets the requirements of the prescribed roof.

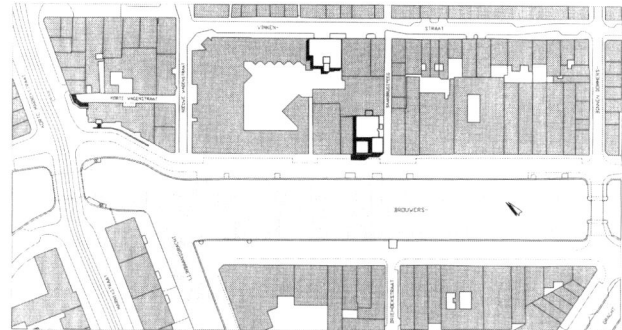

Brouwersgracht and Vinkenstraat

Garden house

The Vinkenstraat was not originally a posh street. It is a street with small industry and cheap houses, and has a less sophisticated rhythm of plots of land than the canals have. Behind the almost thirteen-metre-wide façade is where the members of the commune live. It consists of seven compact apartments and a shared area. For the façade we once again use the masonry turned on its side. We do not divide the façade up, but let the windows of the seven apartments zigzag through the entire surface of the façade to emphasise the unity of the whole complex, but also so that, when you visit another member of the commune, you can enjoy the fact that the light enters the apartment from a slightly different angle. There are two apartments per storey, which share a large balcony. The balconies are staggered above or below one another, which gives you more sunlight and makes it easier to chat with the neighbours above or below you. Marcel Kronenburg has designed a garden house made of plastic corrugated sheeting with an artificial grass floor for the shared area in the transparent hall. From there the residents can enter the grounds of the old people's home De Rietvinck. The members of the commune, who in principle look after themselves, can receive extra assistance there if they need it.

L.A. Rieshuis

The house is named after Leopold Abraham Ries. He occupied a high position in the Ministry of Finance in the Thirties, but he had to resign in 1936 after being arrested on a charge of indecency with a minor. The case attracted a lot of attention in the press. Ries was eventually released and went to the United States shortly before the outbreak of World War II. He died there in 1962. His rehabilitation was a long time coming. When the first stone of the L.A. Rieshuis was laid on 16 October 1997, Ms Borst, Minister of Health, announced on behalf of the government that L.A. Ries had been rehabilitated – a moving moment for the gay community. The L.A. Rieshuis attracts a lot of attention from the radio, television and newspapers. A journalist from the daily newspaper *Trouw* asks me what is different about this project. 'Nothing', I reply. 'It is just an attractive and comfortable house for seven elderly people who have special ties with one another.'

39. Brouwersgracht
    Façade on the run
40. The rhythm of the canal houses
    Entrance with studio
    canal house
41. Stepped balconies
    L.A. Rieshuis
    Entrance L.A. Rieshuis
42. Arched roof canal house

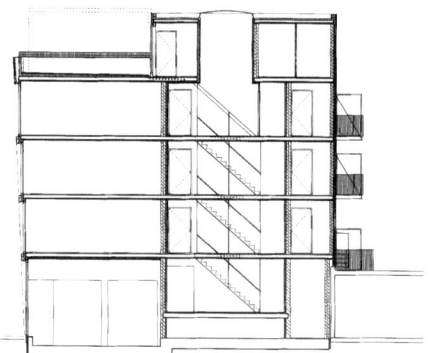

Section canal house

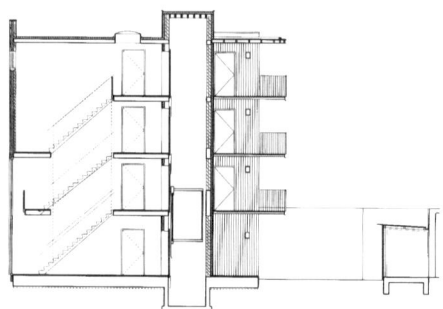

Section L.A. Rieshuis

Canal wall Brouwersgracht

Architecture for me is: atmospheres, images, forms, materials, sounds, scents, landscapes and ideas. I pick up a lot of inspiration during what are often long trips through Europe, North America, South America and Asia, and of course in the architectural practice of Mecanoo. But inextricably intertwined with all that run the memories from my past, such as moving house many times. I always loved moving house: a new house, new surroundings, new worlds. I never missed the previous house. The experience of having lived in different cities and landscapes is also a major source of inspiration — hence this story.

Flat Modern

There are two photos of houses in my parents' home. One is of the house that they had built themselves, the other is of Flat Modern. My parents always told us exciting stories about Flat Modern, a former station hotel in the Stationsstraat in Sittard. It was turned into a block of flats after the war because of the housing shortage. The rooms of the hotel were unusually large for a block of flats. They were even so big that one of the residents always drove his most precious

Flat Modern, Sittard

Twelve houses and a hotel

House and studio, Rotterdam

possession, his car, into the living room. The former bathroom served as a kitchen. My parents were the only ones fortunate enough to own a fridge. The other residents shared this treasure. Sometimes this created confusing situations, like the time when my mother had put some breast milk in the fridge for a moment and one of the other occupants used it in the coffee.

Six round holes

My third house is the one my parents had built in Heerlen in 1959. I remember walking over the site holding my father's hand. Usually my mother did these kinds of things. She discussed with the architect, she bargained with the sub-contractor. My father had every confidence in her. It was a typical Fifties house, a composition of rough natural stone, brick in a white wash, wooden panelling and steel frames. A large and long concrete balcony ran the entire length of the house. The bedrooms were named after the colour of the linoleum on the floor. My sister and I shared the blue room. In the kitchen we had a fantastic Bruynzeel unit with bright colours: red, blue, yellow and black. A free-standing stairway stood in an enormous hall — without storm doors. The balusters had small blobs like music notes. Of course, they were painted red, blue and yellow too. You had to be careful, if you put your head between these balusters to look down, it might get stuck. When you were older, you couldn't get your head between them. The big blue steel front door in the hall with six round holes in it was impressive too. It always suggested to me that I would get another younger brother or sister. There were five of us children.

Building of house, Heerlen

On the scooter

The nice thing about moving house often is that the different houses are connected with different stages in your life. The Limburg hills made a big impression on me. I remember that, when I was four, I didn't dare to go down a slope because I found it too steep. When I went back later, it turned out to be a mound less than a metre high.

I know The Hague mainly from the scooter. I scooted to school via the enlarged ribbon park of the Van Hoogenhoucklaan and Arensdorp Park. I crossed at Oud's Shell building. My youngest brother and I always went to the Hubertus Park. We threw our scooters down below the steps in what we regarded as an enormous dune and raced one another up the steps to the panoramic platform on top. It had a view of the whole of The Hague.

Back door

My fifth house is in Groningen. I lived in the wonderful surroundings of Helpman in a Thirties semi-detached house with a big garden. There were a lot of rooms in the house. The rooms were a bit dark, but that didn't really matter very much. I was always outdoors – on the way to school, playing sports, in the street, in the garden, or in the sports fields near the school. We had a big house but we lived in the kitchen. You always entered the house through the back door. I can't remember ever going in through the front door.

Noise barrier

My eighth house is alongside the busiest railway line in the Netherlands. Less than fifteen metres away, the trains thundered over a concrete viaduct that had been thought up in the Sixties by proud civil engineers. The view from the three windows on the first floor was broken by stripes of Dutch Rail yellow and the Prinsenhof in Delft. They were old sliding windows without double glazing. At the time the whole street protested against the building of a noise barrier which the Law on Noise Pollution laid down. We won. You lived here precisely because you preferred not to live in a cramped street with neighbours on the other side and because it gave you a view over the city. The train was a part of the deal. Very dynamic. It gave me the feeling that you could take the train to Paris just like that.

This old residence was used differently each time. First two families lived in it, then a commune. Then when everyone wanted to live more privately again, the house was turned into three individual units. At a certain moment a part of the house was converted into a firm of architects. We kept on making changes to the house to adapt it to our latest insights and expectations for the future.

1. *Entrance*
2. *Garage*
3. *Studio*
4. *Shower*
5. *Terrace*
6. *Garden*
7. *Living room*
8. *Kitchen*
9. *Balcony*
10. *Bamboo screen*
11. *Library*
12. *Bedrooms*
13. *Void*

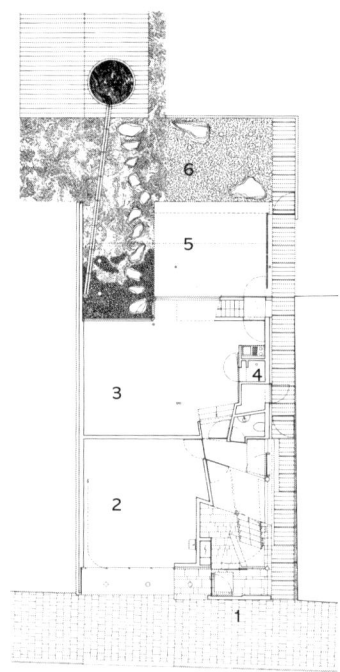

Ground floor

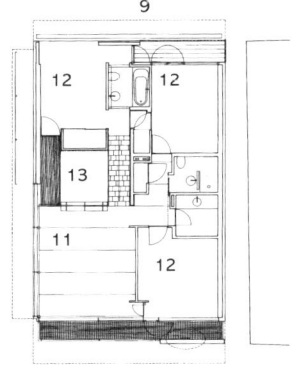

Second floor

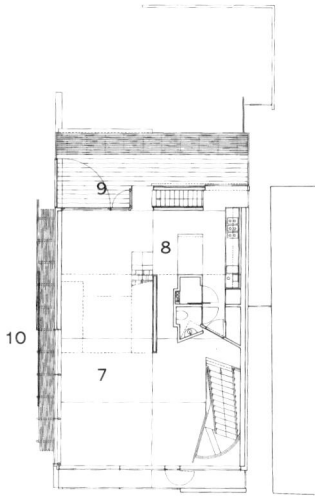

First floor

Nomad

My ninth house is a loft in Rotterdam. I felt like a nomad who spends most of her time working, travelling and staying in hotels a lot. This loft was the ideal place for me. Plenty of room and the bare necessities like a bed, a comfortable chair, a table and a TV. That was all. I usually ate out. The wide Vierambachtstraat with trams and many kinds of foreign shops emphasised my feeling of being a free metropolitan.

Dutch skies

My eleventh house is a flat on the eleventh floor, with a view through nine metres of glass. Delft-Zuid. A Seventies concrete standard high-rise district which everyone who doesn't live there complains about. Nonsense. It was a wonderful apartment. A well-designed ground plan with sliding doors between the rooms. All very compact. You could connect all the rooms with one another. My oldest daughter learned to walk here. She raced through the house on her cross-bike. When we wanted to go to the slide, we took the lift down to go to the playground. The view was fabulous. Once again the luxury of no neighbours facing you, watching the sun, rain and storm passing over the Dutch landscape and making out the lighthouses of the Hook of Holland and Scheveningen on the horizon.

Bamboo screen

Now I live in my twelfth house. You can see the eleven previous ones in it. It was designed to be able to see the Dutch landscape and the Dutch skies.
All the rooms are interconnected by doors that look like panels. The children bike and play all over the house. My bedroom is designed like a hotel room. There are different levels not only in the house but also in the garden. The house is a composition of different materials: natural stone, concrete, glass, steel, wood. Hard and soft, simple and expensive, but always beautiful. It is a house with a front door, a back door and even a side door. It is a house to live, work and play in. The view of the northern side of the lake gives you a sense of being on holiday. In the studio on the ground floor you are a part of a closed, balanced Japanese garden. A zinc fence reflects the waving bamboo. A small swimming pool has been made in the wooden platform above the ditch. If you pull the plug out, the water runs into the ditch. The details of the house make you feel a part of the outside world while you are inside. Only a sheet of glass protects you from rain, wind and unwanted visitors. The moving bamboo screen regulates light, sun and privacy, so that the house not only radiates an atmosphere of openness, but also creates a mood of intimacy inside.

47. *North wall by night*
48. *Composition materials, children in swimming pool*
49. *Library with view over the water*
    Living room level with view of garden
    Living room level with view of water
50. *The movable bamboo screen*
    Studio with view of ditch and garden

Adventure

A total of twelve houses and a hotel. I have not described all of them. They are important to me. They make me oppose the dogmatic and no-risk way in which a single image of a house is dictated by the regulations and the market parties: a house with a garden in a residential neighbourhood. I like houses in busy, noisy and dynamic parts of the city, high-rise flats with a view that are also suitable to live in with children, lofts, apartments with big halls and above all no storm doors, residences that you can occupy in different ways each time, houses with front doors at the back, and industrial premises that can be turned into surprising homes. I love introverted and extroverted neighbourhoods, exciting and boring ones, in the city and in the suburbs. And sometimes with small, rolling hills, even if they are only a metre high.

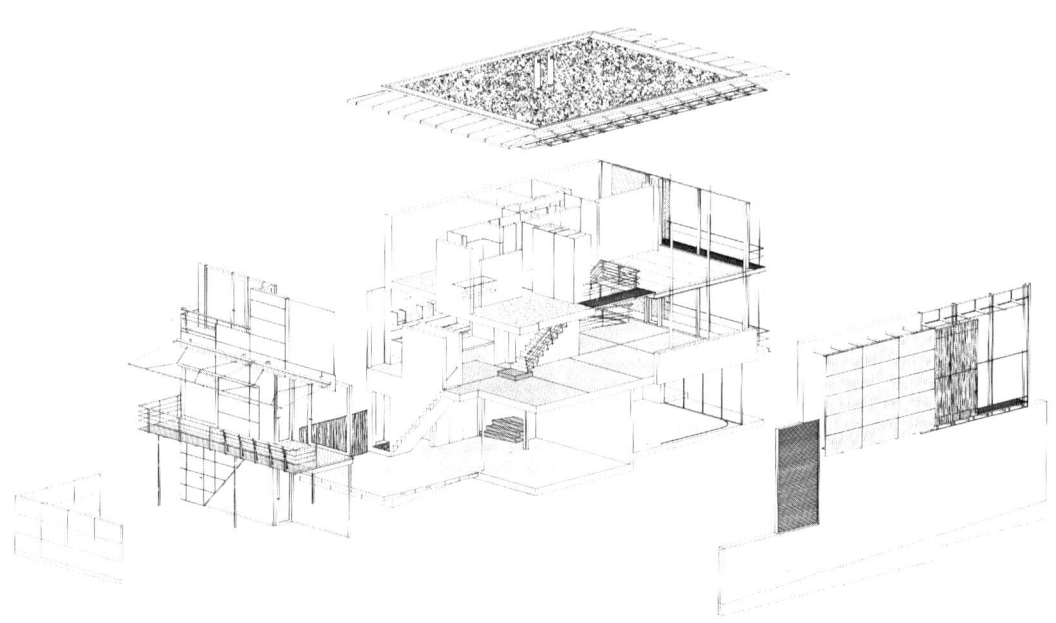

Exploded View

48

In the autumn of 1989 Peter van der Gugten, director of the Social Housing Company, called to ask me to draw up an urban development plan for 550 houses in Prinsenland, the new garden city of Rotterdam. We had previously carried out the Kruisplein youth housing project and the Tiendplein project together, both in the Oude Westen urban renewal district of Rotterdam. Prinsenland is on the outskirts. It used to be a rural area with attractive ribbon buildings, adjacent to the Alexanderpolder postwar residential neighbourhood. The skyline is determined on the one hand by small-scale ribbon development with trees, old farms, houses and villas, and on the other by the monotonous flats of the Alexanderpolder.

Garden city

Our assignment for the Ringvaartplasbuurt Oost consists mainly of council housing, while mainly owner-occupied property is built in the surrounding new estates. The number of housing units per hectare is higher for council housing than for the private sector.

Dancing blocks

The zoning plan speaks of a garden city that must be urban at the same time. And urban is associated with austere and stony.

What is a garden city nowadays, and what is urban? Sometimes I think that urban developers and administrators are frightened to make something non-urban, something informal, something on a village scale. Does what was once a rural setting with its characteristic parcels of land not call for a less monolithic approach and a friendly image instead of city design?

Educational

Garden cities sprang up on a large scale in the Netherlands in the early 1990s. This trend coincided with the shift from building large quantities of rented homes to a primarily owner-occupier market. It marked a rupture in the tradition of Dutch housing which had been orientated towards council housing ever since 1901 and now suddenly had to become market-orientated. In practice it is as if the idea of a garden city is a synonym for houses with a saddle roof, garden, a car parked in front, and a plot of land that is too small. It is as if we have suddenly forgotten the rich international tradition of garden cities in the Netherlands, Germany and England, which had not only a distinctive architecture but also splendid shared gardens. Attractive garden cities are based on an ideology, which is why they have an educational aspect. That is what I want too, but in my own way.

Ringvaartplasbuurt Oost,
Prinsenland, Rotterdam

Tactile quality

In designing a garden city, a tree may be more important in my eyes than a brick. The feeling of a garden city resides not in the sloping roof of the house but in the tactile quality of the neighbourhood. I want to create a district with a high tactile factor, not just in the architecture but also in the public space. I want a neighbourhood that you no longer forget if you grow up there as a child, the period in which you develop your senses. I do not want a neighbourhood filled with concrete 30 x 30 cm city paving stones, but one with a variety of materials, textures, scents and colours; a neighbourhood where you can enjoy and experience, with a strong narrative imaginative force.

Ideals

I put the ideals of my New Garden City to Peter van der Gugten and tell him that these ideals can only be realised in an integrated assignment. We can only achieve it if we can work together with the client on the urban planning, house typology, choice of materials and landscape all at the same time and on developing a vision for management and supervision. Garden cities in the Netherlands are traditionally very well organised by means of detailed agreements, just as the height of the hedge around a garden is described in allotment complexes. Peter van der Gugten agrees with the vision and the procedure.

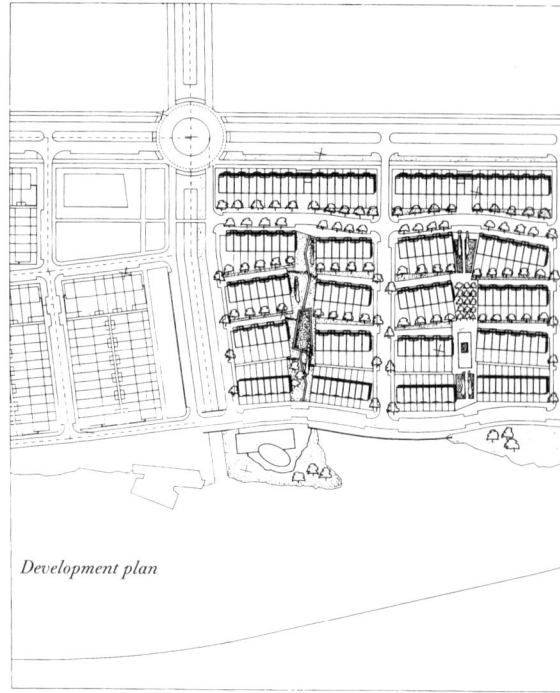

Development plan

Sprayed sand

Nothing is as difficult as designing for a field of sprayed sand, the way in which a location is made ready for building in the Netherlands, with its high water level. There is barely any *genius loci* present. A city has a certain history, other buildings, a lead, something to latch on to or to oppose. There is no complex programme in the case of a sprayed field. While the old garden cities had a collective programme with a baker, a butcher, a church, a community house and a village square, there is none of that in the present-day garden city. The shopping centre and the supermarket are some distance away. The programme covers only the number of housing units, the number of parking lots, and the ground available for them. There are not even any square metres reserved for a communal garden, let alone for a small park.

Ringvaartplas

The Ringvaartplas is created to form a transition between the old ribbon housing of farms and villas and the new district. I want this lake to make its presence felt throughout the plan, but above all not as the modern architects do it, with buildings at right angles to the water. This makes it look as though everyone has a view, which is very democratic. Or does no one have a view?

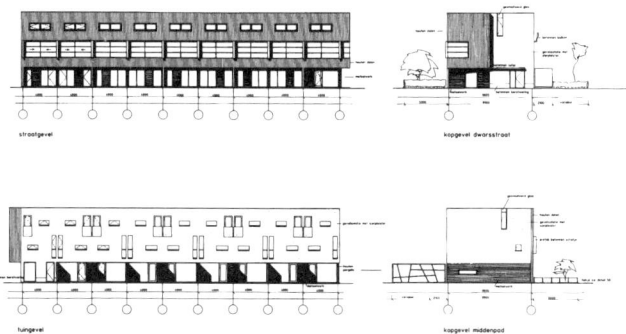

Residential path homes

Lakeside homes

Composition

We have constructed the Ringvaartplasbuurt Oost from four identical quadrants, each with a green backbone. A fifth, non-matching quadrant is marked by a high, collective block of flats. The neighbourhood evokes strong points of reference. The tall block of flats, that marks the neighbourhood like a church tower, seems to rise like a ship in a sea of low-rise buildings. The straight line of buildings along the Jacques Dutilhweg fulfils the role of a dyke behind which the garden city rolls down to the lake. The strict division of the land into strips is transformed into an architectural choreography in which the carefully detailed blocks of flats are the gracious dancers, creating new spaces each time through their change of direction. The residential paths run between the strips, interrupted by the four collective gardens, each in a different style: French, Dutch, Japanese and English.

Living in a cavity

The buildings beside the edge of the lake are on a narrower strip of land than has been conventional in Rotterdam. This releases square metres for the collective gardens. In the town hall they joke about living in a cavity. This enables each quadrant to have its own green backbone, with the different houses grouped around it. Immediately adjacent to the lake are the Plasrandwoningen (Lakeside homes). These are extremely narrow, tall flats which begin on the first floor, offering a splendid view of the lake. Immediately behind them are the Woonpadwoningen (Residential path homes). These are somewhat wider two-storey flats with a cap-shaped roof, thereby creating an attic in the house. The flats that stand strictly to attention and form the back of the quadrant are two-storey flats with low apartments on top of them. They have a shared front door right in the middle of the block at the end of the green backbone, which connects them with the lake.

Sheds

To achieve the image of a green, luxuriant garden city, the private gardens are not fenced off by bike sheds, as is the case with the traditional division of streets in the Netherlands. All of the bike sheds have been incorporated in the flats. The private gardens and the collective gardens determine the green image of this garden city, that recalls J.J.P. Oud's wonderful combination of gardens and architecture in the low-rise flats in the Weissenhofsiedlung in Stuttgart.

Step by step

The paths leading to the flats are a car-free zone, suitable for young children on tricycles or scooters or for playing marbles, just in view of the home. The collective gardens are for the slightly older children, away from the direct vision of their parents. They gradually explore the larger playing fields beside the lake and the Dutilhweg before coming to discover the whole city as their playground when they are adolescents.

The composition of buildings in this neighbourhood and the variety of urban space can be interpreted as a manifesto against the monotony and against the lack of interest in public space in urban expansion schemes of this kind.

Different landscapes

The French, Dutch, Japanese and English landscape styles determine the design of the four gardens. Paving, street furniture, play objects, plants and trees are selected in accordance with these themes. If you ride over the path of concrete blocks that are sunk into the grass of the Japanese garden on your tricycle, you hear not only the bumping noise of your tricycle but also the rustling of the bamboo. You can climb on the large, angular rocks and play with the flat gravel. In the English garden you can skate on the winding path between the gently rolling hills, play miniature golf, and prick yourself on the stuffy roses. If you climb onto the farmyard fences in the Dutch garden with its pollard willows you can see black and white cows and a red bull. In the French garden you can play on old paving stones beneath a roof of pollard sycamore leaves. Further on is a big sand pit, with Parisian benches around it and a fence to keep the dogs out. It has all been devised with children in mind, but it is also simply attractive when the children no longer live there. You can smell the spring. You can see the colours of autumn. You can experience the changes of the seasons.

Materials and colours

White stucco on the south side, a range of terracotta-like colours on the north side. A combination of wooden and masonry roof gables and a window that cuts through both materials. A plinth of black blocks of concrete. A concrete and glass screen for privacy. And as an extra detail a specially designed prefab concrete garden bench that can be turned into a storage chest or a rabbit cage. The expressive concrete caps of the Residential path homes. The rhythm of the piers that function as fire-walls between the room-wide windows on the first floor of the Lakeside homes. The wooden ship's railings of the corridors. The clock and the flagpole on the ship. Architecture can be tactile. A building can tell stories. You can feel a material.

---

55. *View of Lakeside homes seen over the Ringvaartplas*
56. *Collage Japanese garden*
    Collage French garden
57. *Scale model of the Ship*
    View of the Ringvaartplasbuurt Oost
58. *Detail of Japanese garden*
59. *North wall of the Ship*
60. *The English garden*
62. *Side view of Residential path homes*

56

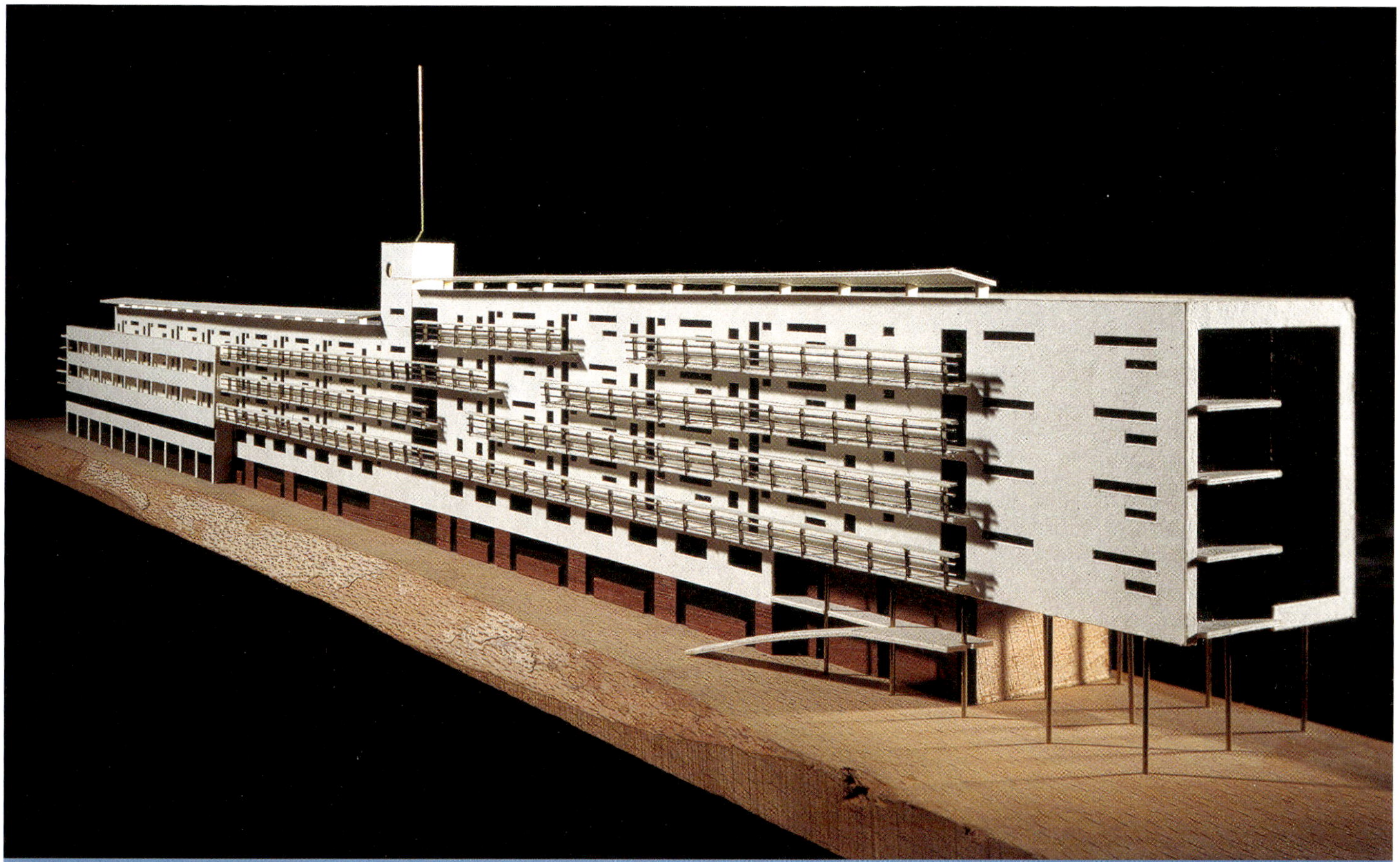

Werkgroep 5x5

In the spring of 1989 Iepke Gietema, councillor for Town and Country Planning, and Niek Verdonk, director of Town Development, ask me to make a master plan for the public areas in the historic city centre. I know them from Werkgroep 5x5, a working committee that was set up in 1987 in reaction to Dutch housing policy. It was an initiative of Adri Duivesteijn and Willem Gieczenman. After the event 'Urban renewal as a cultural activity' has been successfully concluded in The Hague, they think that something national has to be done. 'Regulations have replaced inspiration in housing. Bureaucracy directs and suffocates culture. Quantity instead of quality has set the tone in this country for too long. What has also paralysed practically everyone involved in housing is the realisation of being personally responsible.' These criticisms are from the Appeal of 16 May 1988. This manifesto criticises conventional practice and gives the signal for a new élan. It is signed by some forty signatories. The members are kindred spirits (councillors, architects, artists, representatives of tenants organisations and clients) who work in five disciplines connected in some way with housing, and they come from five different cities. This is the origin of the working committee and the name: Werkgroep 5x5. The name not only indicates its origin, but also suggests an optimistic future. The message of 5x5 can be extended indefinitely: 5x5x5x5x5...

Space for space

Reorganisation of public space, Groningen city centre

Daily work

A large event is held in Rotterdam from 22 to 24 November 1989: the three days of the Housing Week. Old and new ambitions, fine words and stubborn realities meet in the same arena. Werkgroep 5x5 dissolves itself after this event. This is not because its work is over, but because it only wanted to initiate a process of change. Qualities cannot be separated out in institutions or working committees. Quality should be a part of daily work. From now on the full responsibility for achieving quality lies in everyone's daily work. This two-year period of intensive discussions, meetings, excursions and late-night conversations in the pub sees the rise of connections and friendships which, as later transpires, are extremely useful in making the search for new ambitions a success.

Space for space

When Iepke Gietema and Niek Verdonk make their request, neither they nor we have a clear objective in mind. The most essential thing is the theme of 'space for space': attention and funding for the public space. It is the time of the successful renewal of Barcelona, a strategy to breathe new life into the city by renovating its many squares. These interventions are wonderfully conceived and have a high design content. The authorities expect that we might design a typically Groningen clock, or a wonderful steel or wooden bench, but our approach is very different. Together with designer Chris Emar and other civil servants from the Groningen local authority, we embark on a quest for a balance between structure and meaning in the open space, for functional effectiveness and spatial quality. We drive to Groningen and back every week.

Detail of the Alcázar in Sevilla

Barcelona and Seville

In June 1989 I am in Barcelona, the model city that has shown that brightening up the public space is a major stimulus to the city. Most of the squares are beautiful, pure architectural objects that are viable on the hard Spanish ground, but not on the feeble Dutch soil.
In September 1989 I am in Seville. I am moved by the beauty of the Alcázar because of the calm it radiates, the wonderful patios of yellow petrified soil, with a narrow blue border of mosaic around them. The public space does not compete with the architecture, but fills the surrounding buildings with its calm and simplicity. That is what we must try to find for the historic city centre of Groningen.

The Expressive City

Total plan

Groningen has a lovely old city centre with a clear spatial structure of streets and squares, surrounded by a ring of canals. In the last few decades, however, this structure has become hidden from view by shop displays, bike racks, rubbish containers, glass containers, advertising signs and terraces. The Traffic Circulation Plan of 1976 was an attempt to reduce motorised traffic and to strengthen the housing function of the city centre. This led to a surfeit of traffic signs and parking prevention bollards. They make the visual pollution of the public space even worse. Instead of being bothered by cars, pedestrians and cyclists are now bothered by all the devices to keep cars out. We see it as our task to bring clarity and calm to the look of the city with a total plan for the public space. After three years of discussions with politicians, civil servants, associations of shopkeepers, catering concerns and residents, we reach agreement on the wishes, possibilities and criteria for the restructuring of the centre. In 1991 we present the master plan 'Space for Space' in which the city is divided up into four different 'cities' that overlap, merge and combine to form a whole. They are the Controlled City, the Characteristic City, the Expressive City, and the Hidden City.

The Controlled City

Controlled City

The Controlled City is the neutral network of streets, squares, passageways and alleys, the city structure as it has existed for centuries. The view of this structure has become increasingly cloudy over the years because of the more and more intensive use of the city centre. The purpose of the master plan is to make the structure of the city recognisable again. The restructuring itself is carried out with modest resources. The key words in this restructuring process are: coherence and continuity, unity in diversity, beauty through simplicity.

Characteristic City

The Characteristic City is the city of the postcards, the places that stick in the memory of residents and visitors. It is they and not other points that determine the image of Groningen. In the Characteristic City Groningen distinguishes itself from other cities: Grote Markt, Vismarkt, and the ring of canals. The arrangement of the Characteristic City must fit in with the arrangement of the Controlled City, emphasise the special character of the location, and solve the site-specific problems.

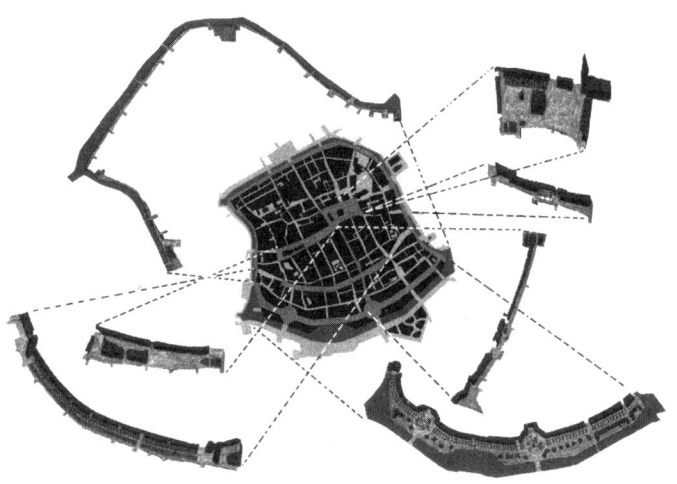

The Characteristic City

Hidden City

The Hidden City consists of the public areas that are out of sight of the urban structure of the Controlled City. These courtyards and gardens lead an introverted, 'quiet' life, far from the bustle and constantly changing image of the city. You do not come across the Hidden City in everyday use of the city, it is difficult to find. Little has changed in the Hidden City in the course of centuries. There is no reason at all to change any of it at the moment.

Expressive City

The Expressive City indicates those rare points where an exuberant design of the public space is in place. This is where the city radiates its vitality and élan. The sites of the Expressive City, indicated with asterisks on the map, have often been bottlenecks in the city for years. A well thought out intervention in the Expressive City will benefit the whole of Groningen. The principles of this approach are: strengthening of the spatial quality, utilisation of opportunities, resolution of bottlenecks in use. This is where an exuberant, trendy style of building can and should add an extra spatial quality to the city, without disrupting the Controlled or the Characteristic City.

Scoria bricks

The Controlled City is the basis for the organisation of the public space that must be simple, modest and of a high quality and must confer calm and unity on the image of the city. This basis must be capable of lasting for years, surviving intensive use, and not subject to fashion. The street materials are new, yellow baked bricks with lines of old, shiny granite pebbles and smooth, blue scoria bricks for emphasis. This wonderful collection of old stones that have been lying at various points in the city for years is not suitable for whole streets; they are scarce and it is not very comfortable to walk on them. We use them for essential detail, the contrasting effect, and the reflection of the light when it is raining or when evening falls. The street materials are the same all over the Controlled City. They are formed by a beautiful combination of contrasts between old and new, the large surface area and the long line, light and dark colours, matt and shiny.

Conditions

The restructuring of the Controlled City is the basis of the master plan 'Space for Space'. That is also what we concentrate on the most. We lay down three conditions: the plan is only worthwhile if the proposals are carried out in an integrated fashion; if common interest prevails over sectoral interest; and if pedestrians and cyclists have priority in the circulation of traffic. We issue far-reaching proposals for the restructuring of the Controlled City. The plans cover bringing the circulation of traffic into line with the structure of the city, no illogical one-way traffic, no irritating barriers, proposals for bike sheds, street materials and profiles, lights, trees and the addition of greenery, street furniture, terraces and shop displays, and the application of art in the public space. This is a hierarchical list. In weighing up the different components, the circulation of traffic is the most important, while art is the least important.

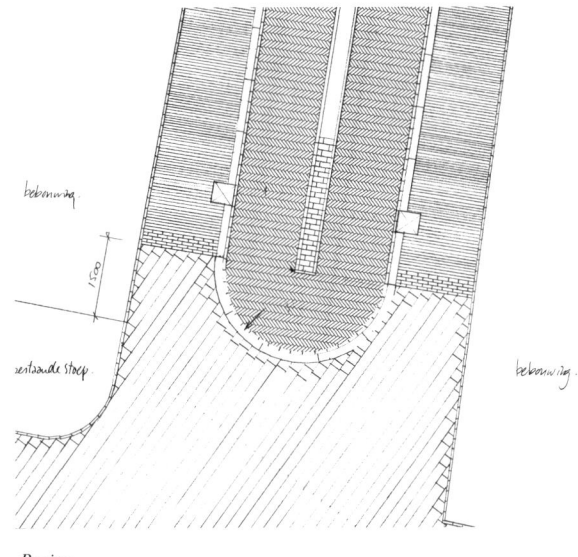

Paving

Management

'Space for Space' is an integrated plan for the whole of the city centre of Groningen. It attempts to offer a solution for everything that goes on in the public space. The master plan envisages an intensive management of the public space and supervision of the use laid down in the design. The execution of the master plan will take fifteen years. It has its own project organisation. We have produced the *Space for Space Manual* for that purpose, which includes the main profiles of the streets, the street material and a checklist of conditions for use that each part of the design must satisfy. Management, maintenance and supervision are also covered in it: the management of the Controlled City.

Pilot

At the same time as the master plan we develop the public space of one of the most complex parts of the city centre of Groningen as a pilot project: Poelestraat and Peperstraat and environs. It is the centre for going out where there are major conflicts of interest not only between the daytime and the nighttime catering establishments, but also between the shopkeepers and the residents. The pilot project helps us to see whether our ideas work, and whether the material we choose really does the job. For instance, we had originally thought of firing the stones a bronze-coloured green, but this proved to be technically impossible. As the area is a part of the Controlled City, it must be given a neutral design. The street is a single surface from wall to wall. The line of scoria bricks, at a distance from the wall, brings structure to this surface. Between this line and the wall is a zone that can be used as a terrace by those who use the premises. This part consists of clinkers laid in stretcher bond at right angles to the wall. The rest of the surface consists of stones of a larger format that are laid diagonally to the wall. This makes the public space an autonomous area, independent of the alignment of the walls.

Barcelona in Seville

The terrace in the middle of the Poelestraat is a part of the Expressive City. It has rising terraces that reveal the difference in level of the Hondsrug where the centre of Groningen was founded in 1040. A steel pergola has been constructed above the terrace as an allusion to the old city gate that used to stand here. This architectural object is the most striking but least interesting part of the design. The expressive style is a deliberate choice: it gives identity to the location and has become an attractive terrace for the people of Groningen to enjoy. It can take root in the memory of the townspeople and live for ever, or it may be replaced by another architectural object in ten years' time. The great importance of the pilot project for the design of the entire public area lies in cleaning up the streets and the square, and showing the need to design a peaceful public space with extreme precision. The object is like a piece of Barcelona in Seville.

67. *Street views*
68. *Terrace Poelestraat*
69. *Details of paving*
70. *Street views*

70

Entrance to a city farm in the city of Maastricht

Maastricht is a beautiful city in the south of the Netherlands. It is the city of the attractive squares, old walls, churches, monasteries, city farms, and the elegant use of artisanal materials. It is the most Burgundian, medieval, monumental and beautifully situated city in the Netherlands, on the banks of the River Meuse in the rolling hills of Limburg. The city is expanding within its own borders to protect the surrounding landscape as much as possible. This is the result of an exemplary policy under former director of Urban Development Huub Smeets. The former councillor John Weevers shows me the old inner area between the Brusselsestraat and the Calvariestraat. It is one of the 5x5 locations. My Limburg background and surname come in useful in Maastricht.

Intimacy and reconciliation

Herdenkingsplein
[Commemorative Square], Maastricht

Postmodern

The first confrontation with the location and with the urban development plan of the local authority is a strange and confusing experience. It is a unique and barely accessible area with a semi-functioning industrial site, a block of flats, a concrete school building and lots of parked cars. It looks like an amorphous mass that has absolutely no relation with its surroundings. The local authority's urban development plan shows a large square with a circular wall next to a small tower; beneath the square is a large underground car park, which makes a lot of sense in this setting. It is a formal idiom that makes a very strange impression on us in this medieval city. Why such a big square with the pretentious name Herdenkingsplein (Commemoration Square) on this location? A further complication is the fact that there are three architects, each with their own client and assignment: Wiel Arets for the Art Academy; Boosten/Rats for the car park and some of the flats; and Mecanoo for the design of the square and the rest of the housing.

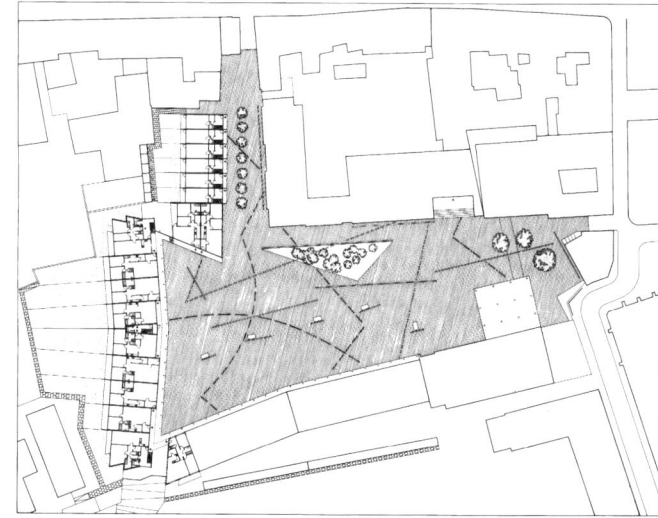

Public nature and intimacy

The many round gateways in the neighbouring streets recall the numerous city farms that used to be found in this area. The animals have gone and all kinds of businesses have taken over the land. The farmyards and buildings were then demolished, while the gateways and the houses that line the streets are still there. What was originally the most intimate part of the area is exposed by projecting a public square there. We will play on this opposition. The interaction between intimate and public becomes the theme of the plan. It is the basis for the shape of the square, the introduction of the colonnade, the layered construction of the walls, and the use of materials.

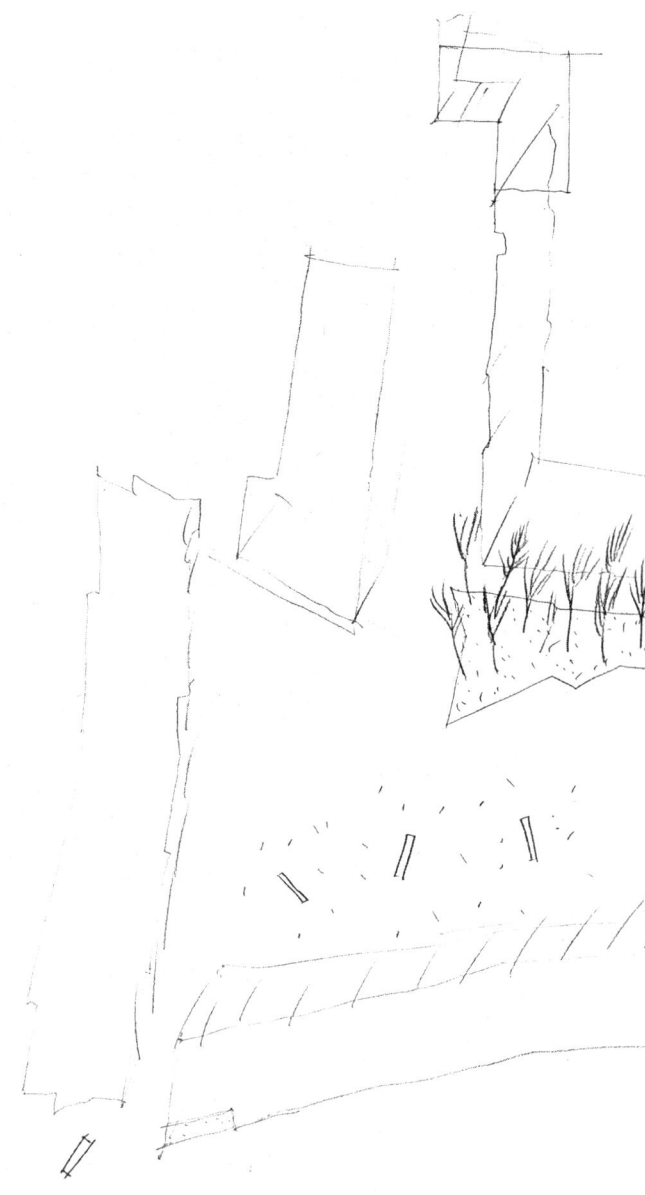

Sketch of the new plan for the square

Reconciliation

The present-day square is an interruption in the medieval network of the city. The contours of the square are buckled, sometimes symmetrically and sometimes not, following the informal routes that give access to the square. These access points have been deliberately kept pinched and narrow so that the square can remain a secret spot in the city. One of the access points is formed by the glass volumes of Wiel Arets' Art Academy. The colonnade with the chiselled natural stone entrance is the dividing line between the public character of the square and the private character of the houses. At the same time it is a way of reconciling the plans of the Boosten/Rats and Mecanoo firms of architects. The colonnade ensures a peaceful, distinguished look. The walls surrounding the square have a formal language of their own – not the sum of the individual homes, but an abstract whole. The homes are situated behind a screen of white varnished western cedar. The detailing of the balconies and corridors makes them barely conspicuous.

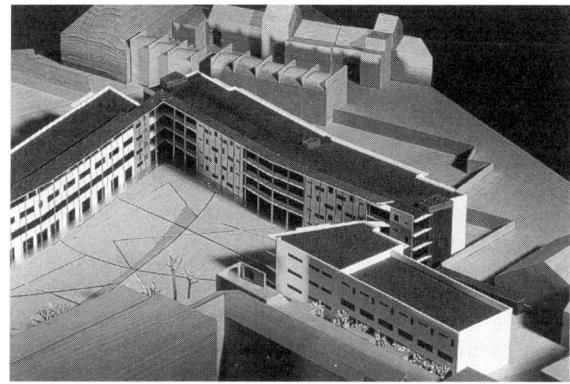

Model Herdenkingsplein

75. *Walls made from the stones of demolished buildings*
    Rear wall with balconies
76. *East and North wall of square*
    Paving (detail)
    Passage to Calvariestraat
77. *Colonnade with chiselled natural stone gallery*
78. *Fragment North wall of square*
    Fragment East wall

Space

We have used stone from the buildings that were demolished in the neighbourhood to finish the staircases at the tops of the blocks of flats. The walls of the gardens and sheds to the rear are also made of these second-stand bricks to interweave the new project with the look of the old city. Traces of stainless steel, corten steel and concrete have been incorporated in the square. They constitute a play of lines in the large surface of granite stones. The character of the square is determined by the art of omission, in combination with high-quality, artisanal materials, resulting in a spatial square full of atmosphere. A few trees correct and soften the contours of the square.

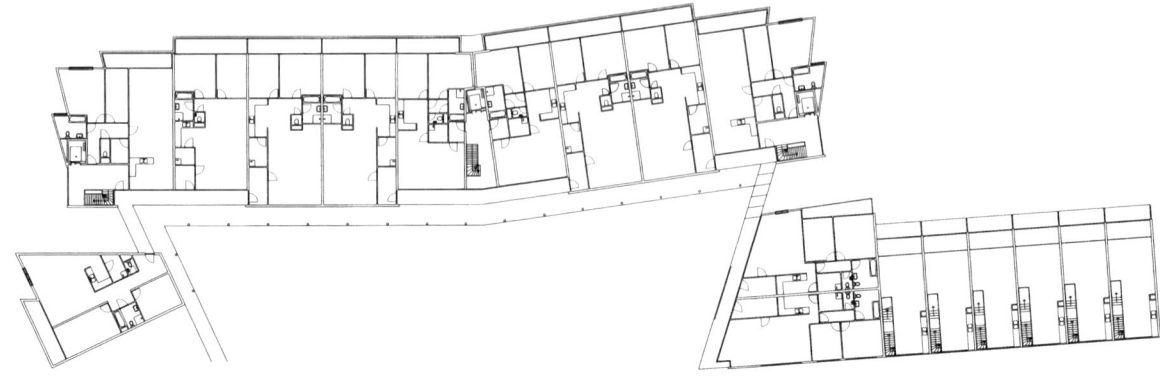

First floor

In 1991 the O.M.A. firm of architects makes a master plan for the university complex De Uithof in Utrecht. This Sixties campus is one of many in the Netherlands, situated outside the city, which have never experienced the enormous growth that was predicted at the time. De Uithof consists of detached, mainly concrete buildings scattered among the fields. It is an unattractive, characterless area. The main principle of the master plan is 'the university in the landscape': the whole university complex including future extensions must be kept as compact as possible to retain the openness of the surrounding landscape. The master plan is composed of zones, each with its own identity and rules. The Faculty for Economics and Management is a part of the Kasbah zone, a wide strip with a high density of low, introverted buildings.

A lot on a large scale

The Faculty for Economics and Management has been housed so far in seven different buildings in the inner city. The new building must accommodate five thousand students and four hundred members of staff on a floor surface area of 25,000 m². The programme for the school is dull:

Kasbah in the polder

lots of classrooms, lots of rooms, lots of lecture theatres, a canteen and a media centre, as well as study areas for students – a lot on a large scale with a modest budget. While mediocrity is what we want to avoid. We are the first architects to design a building within the master plan. The location we are given is nondescript.

Kasbah

We investigate the idea of the kasbah, a phenomenon in the history of architecture that received attention in the Sixties with Aldo van Eyck's Orphanage in Amsterdam and the Freie Universität in Berlin by the French architects Candilis and Woods. The latter are convinced that high-rise buildings are not suitable for a democratic university. They associate them with 'insulation layers', where professors and their staff no longer communicate with the floor – that is, the other professors and their staff – above or below them. Low-rise buildings of two or three storeys facilitate an open, accessible, democratic school with a fully-fledged place for the individual. We study, analyse and interpret the kasbah idea in our own way: towns in North Africa that lie as fortresses in the desert. The only striking element in the simple, neutral outer wall is the big door. The town itself contains perfectly detailed and decorated patios that determine the atmosphere of the kasbah. We choose these two readings of the kasbah – democratic and patio – as substantive themes for the design of the faculty building.

Ground plan North African kasbah

Van den Broek and Bakema

In 1976, when we were students at the Delft Technical University, we organised the biennial, by now notorious Stylosfeest. A party for four thousand in the faculty of architecture building designed by Van den Broek and Bakema. It may not be a beautiful building, but it is pre-eminently suitable for studying, giving parties and organising exhibitions. The Stylosfeest was held on the ground floor, the first floor and in the basement. Twenty-one groups performed on six different stages. Two restaurants, a cinema and a disco were organised. At that time, in our second year as students, we were beginning to appreciate the building more and more, particularly because of its pleasant 'gross-nett' factor. No one eats in the canteen, hardly anyone sketches or studies in the study rooms. Everything takes place informally at tables in the hall and in the corridors. That is where the discussions take place, that is where we talk about design, politics and music. Those are the areas that make the school a unity, a source of inspiration.

Circulation

We propose to our clients Harm Noordhof and Diane Kattenkamp to boldly invert the usual proportion between room space, traffic space and outdoor space for the Faculty of Economics and Management. The normal relation between gross and nett surface areas covered in the budget would result in a big school with above all many long corridors, with a lack of orientation, identity or a sense of belonging. The clients realise that and come back a little later with a creative proposal to organise the teaching programme and schedule in a different way. This creates the scope to make a building with the pleasant 'gross-nett' factor that we want. We make a design in which the classrooms and offices are frames for the corridors, halls and patios, instead of the other way around. The life of the faculty will take place in the circulation of the building.

Metropolis

The faculty building is actually an enormous circulation machine in which large numbers of students are continually pumped round for maximal exchange and interaction in learning. The square ground plan, with four connecting parts separated from one another by three patios, ensures a free circulation to every corner of the building. The idea of five thousand students who have to keep changing classroom every fifty minutes recalls images from Fritz Lang's film *Metropolis*: masses of people moving from one place to another. Lifts will never be able to cope with those numbers, so we will have to make a pedestrian building. It becomes a three-storey building with a 1.20 metre difference in level. Each classroom is 20 cm higher than the previous one. Now you can walk effortlessly from one floor to another through the empty spaces, staircases, bridges and slopes. These carefully arranged different levels give the horizontal flows of traffic a vertical twist, so that an intense vertical flow is automatically produced between the three storeys. Steel bridges intersect the Jungle patio so that this outdoor area is also incorporated in the system of circulation. Wouldn't a Faculty for Economics and Management with a building like this immediately radiate more openness?

Ground plan second floor

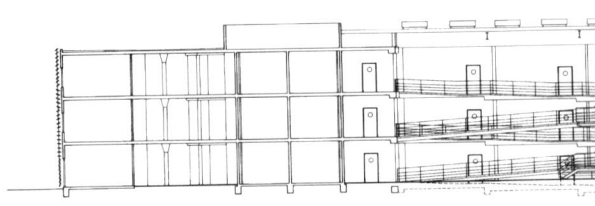

Cross-section of classrooms, left wing

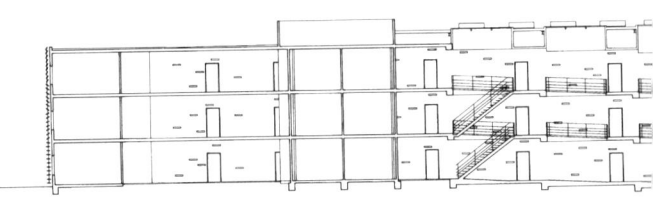

Cross-section of classrooms, right wing

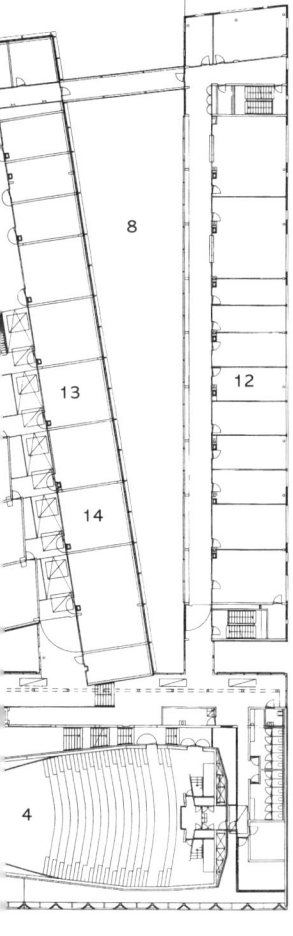

1. *Lecture rooms for 120 people*
2. *Lecture rooms for 90 people*
3. *Lecture room for 150 people*
4. *Lecture room for 400 people*
5. *Classroom for 60 people*
6. *Zen patio*
7. *Jungle patio*
8. *Water patio*
9. *Study squares*
10. *Administrative section*
11. *Slopes*
12. *Computer rooms*
13. *Classroom for 30 people*

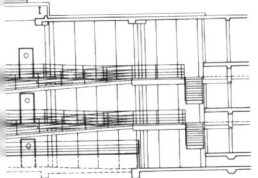

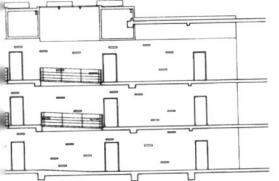

Congress

You must be able to form a good picture of the whole building as soon as you arrive. You must experience the school as a whole in height, breadth and depth. The main entrance is situated on the main boulevard with 'the congress': a collection of lecture rooms in all shapes and sizes, a media centre, and a restaurant. The whole ensemble is designed like a big block of ice. Four large volumes in different shapes and materials are sunk halfway into the ice; concrete legs ensure that they do not go any further. The space beneath and between these closed sculptural boxes with lecture rooms is used for a media centre and a kitchen. This space is also a part of the philosophy by which the gross area of the balconies, corridors and intermediate levels is mainly used informally to eat, study, make contact or just sit and do nothing. And to organise congresses and parties.

Undressed and dressed

The naked framework is veiled and exposed in a refined manner by means of grills. Outer walls of sheet cement are hidden by panels of steel grids, sometimes behind stylised wooden lattices in what appears to be an arbitrary grid pattern or futuristic, movable aluminium strips covering the entire surface of the wall like enormous Venetian blinds. In the corridors the wiring and piping for the technical installations have been covered in places with semi-transparent grids of zinc metal sheeting. Ceilings are only put in when necessary for acoustic reasons. The rough construction, installations and finishing are independent of one another. This renders the emphatically bare and naked character of the whole building both tactile and veiled. Compelled by the limited budget, the building has become a composition with an erotic tension between dressed and undressed.

Three patios

The building has a total of three patios: the Zen patio, the Jungle patio, and the Water patio, each with its own meaning, position and theme. They form the heart of our building and determine the mood, just as in the traditional kasbah the perfectly kept patio and patio walls are the most important elements.

Zen patio

The design of the Zen patio is inspired by Japanese gardens for meditation. The patio is in hard materials. This patio is the most static of the three. The walls lengthwise are fitted with wooden, western red cedar grids to keep out the sun. The Zen patio has two sorts of gravel, twelve enormous rocks and two trees. The two sorts of gravel are placed in parallel lines, so that the length of the patio receives even more emphasis. They differ slightly in colour, but strongly in texture: small moraine pebbles and fine flat gravel (flachkorn). They are separated by a strip of corten steel. There are large reddish-brown blocks of stone in the field of gravel: on one side a group of somewhat smaller ones, and on the other side a group of large square and elongated stones, set horizontally and vertically. The two trees, sophoras, with their green twigs and fine green leaves form an attractive contrast with the stones, the gravel and the wood-panelled wall. You see a different composition every time from the classrooms and offices that enclose it. By night the spotlights placed in a low position produce an exciting scene of illuminated stones and big, dark cast shadows in which the two lighted trees stand.

Jungle patio

This patio has an angular, dynamic shape and is the largest of the three. You can feel the jungle from the terrace and the steel gangways, but you cannot enter it. You can sit on the bronze seats designed and made by the artist Linda Verkaaik. She has pierced the hard grids with steel bamboo shoots and refined the squares of the grids with a colourful mosaic. The real bamboo of different colours and sizes will overrun this bridge in the course of time: nature is victorious in the end! Plants with very large horizontal leaves have also been placed in the jungle to create space. The bamboo makes a pleasant rustling sound at the slightest breeze. At the bend in the gangway are three Japanese nut trees, whose rigid shape contrasts with the movements of the bamboo.

Water patio

The Water patio is the narrowest of the three patios, with a length of seventy metres, and a width which tapers from fourteen to four metres. A glass gangway preserves the transparency in relation to the open landscape with the fields and the willows. The water symbolises the calm within the building. The circle of earth-coloured ceramic that fans out in this reflecting surface is the work of the artist Vera van der Leun. As a reflecting pool, the water makes the area seem larger than it really is. The water reflects the smooth walls, the work of art, and – more important still – the sky. The surface of the water is constantly changing with the changes in the weather. The patio is illuminated at night by underwater lighting from one side. Only a part of the ceramic elements is lit, creating large cast shadows.

Finishing touch

The building process takes a total of twenty-three months. In the twenty-third month the gardener lays the gardens in four weeks. It is a moving moment. The gardens compensate the concrete of the building, warm and cold meet. The patios are finished. The kasbah in the polder is complete. Students and staff can use their faculty.

83. *Main entrance with conference zone*
    Jungle patio with gangway
84. *Conference zone*
85. *Open areas, stairs, bridges and slopes in the classroom wing*
86. *Entrance hall*
    Each classroom is 20 cm higher than the previous one
87. *View of the Zen patio*
    Composition of gravel, stones and trees in the Zen patio
88. *West wall with aluminium panels*
    The terrace and bridges in the Jungle patio
89. *The Water patio with the glass bridge: transparency towards the open landscape*
90. *North wall: the conference zone at night*

Detail decoration of North African patio

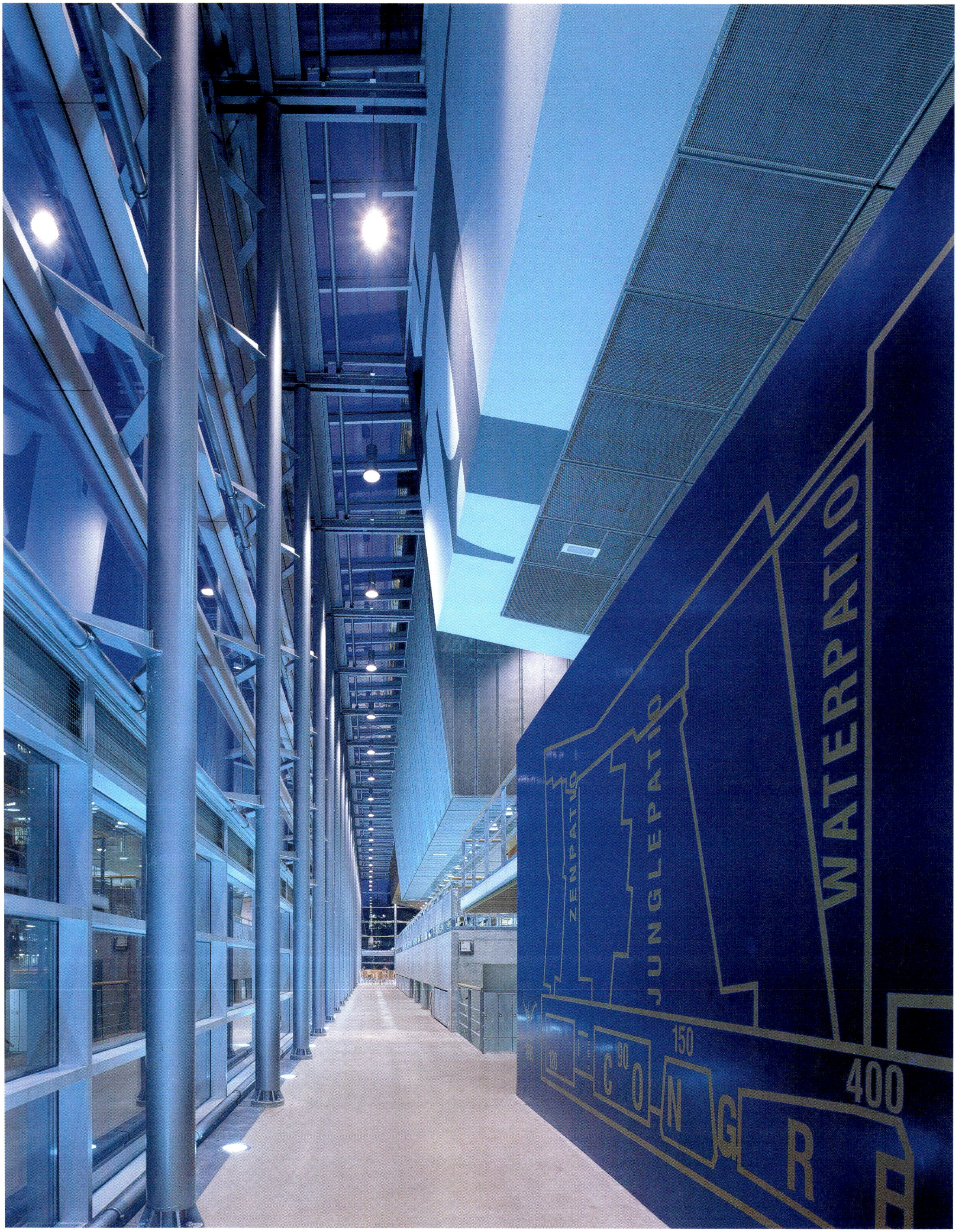
WATERPATIO
JUNGLEPATIO
ZENPATIO
150
400
90
20
C O N G R E

Paddy Tomesen visits his old secondary school and meets his drawing teacher, who tells him that the school has plans for new premises. The choice of the architect has almost been settled. There are three candidates left. Paddy explains enthusiastically that he is on trainee placement with Mecanoo architects and leaves some journals with our work behind. The next day, as we are working late at night on a scale model for a competition, he tells us about the building plans of his old secondary school. He casually inquires whether we are interested. The next day he phones the drawing teacher and arranges a meeting with the school. Two days later – it is spring 1990 – I meet director Lex Drosten and his Building Commission in the Tiendplein in Rotterdam.

School of the senses

Six years later, on 13 December 1996, we are awarded the School Building Prize for the best-looking school in the Netherlands.

Oude IJssel
The Isala College in Silvolde is situated in an idyllic location in the Paasberg nature reserve in the eastern part of the Netherlands. The Oude IJssel, the stream from which the school takes its name, flows in the distance parallel to a sand path with old oaks. I know the Oude IJssel very well. My grandfather was village doctor in the region. He brought a whole generation of villagers into the world, including the school porter. As a child I used to go swimming in the Oude IJssel with my cousins. We rowed in makeshift boats and went on adventurous expeditions along the river banks. The iron foundries date from the period when ore was found in the soil. The small artisanal brick kilns that made bricks from the red clay have been closed down by now.

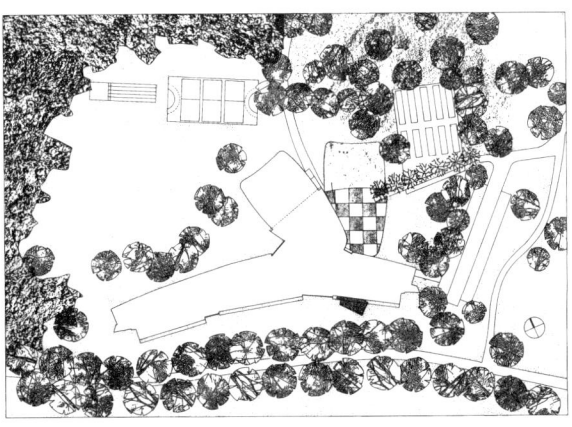

Isala College, Silvolde

Temporary accommodation

For almost twenty years the teachers, staff and pupils have been housed in a proliferating complex of temporary buildings that has spread out over the site like a blob. The walking distances are long, and few people enjoy the view of the Paasberg lane. The school site is large. The new building is planned next to the sports fields.

A completely different plan occurs to me. I project the new building plumb next to the oak-lined lane on the exact spot where a large number of barrack-like buildings are standing at the moment. It has to be an elongated building with a gentle curve – as if it follows the bend in the river – and two storeys high, so that you can just see the river landscape of the Oude IJssel below the oak tops.

Building freeze

The location of the new building is a difficult decision for the school. It means that the pupils and teachers will have to leave the temporary barracks and find alternative accommodation for two years while building goes on. They agree all the same. It only means adding another two years to the twenty years of temporary barracks. Afterwards they will be in the most beautiful location for the next hundred years!

A building freeze of three years is imposed on the school during the design process. We use this time to work out the programme, flexibility, construction, location and choice of materials down to the last detail. It is a good thing not to design and build too quickly. A design needs time to develop and crystallise. The client has to prepare for it and be able to think about whether it fits the future changes in education. Is this the school we want?

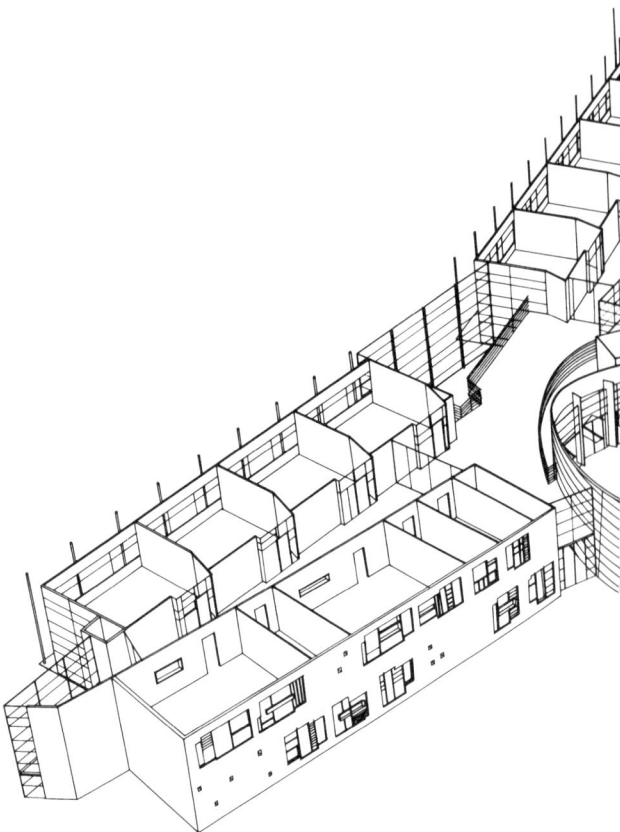

Axonometry

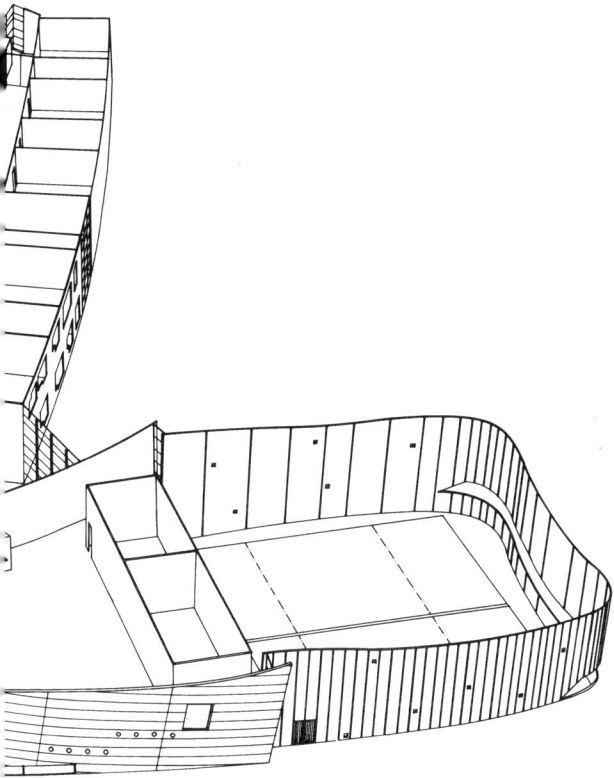

Perforations

Seated in the calm, sober classrooms, the pupils can let their thoughts wander over the rolling landscape. Sometimes someone out for a stroll passes by. The untreated concrete walls in the classroom reveal the construction that has to carry the weight of the building. A low concrete wall follows the corridor on the northeast side. Behind it are the special subject rooms, each of a different size. Perforations have been made in the concrete wall like showcases. A violin, a sculpture, glass jars, old maps: the objects in the showcase show which subject is involved. Music, drawing, engineering, handicrafts, physics, chemistry, biology, geography, history. The corridor is wide and has a warm colour. The staircases, open areas and glass fronts of the special subject rooms prevent you from losing touch with the surrounding landscape. Hanging acoustic ceilings and small ventilation hatches are almost invisible solutions to the problems of noise levels and fresh air that are so important to the functioning of a school. The oak trees form a natural blind, together with the pergola attached to the outer wall.

Train crash

The collective areas intersect the simple, clear part of the school of corridors. The builders refer to the ground plan of the school as a train crash. The dry sandy soil of the site enables us to make a basement. The cloakroom, hall and gym programme is carried out at split level with the school corridors. The light falls through the roof into the basement where 800 pupils can hang up their coats. The hall and the half sunken, double gym form the heart of the school. It is an intelligently designed, complex, multifunctional intersection: this is where plays are staged, sports days are organised, exams are held, and concerts and parties are organised. Every day you can eat your sandwiches beneath a rippling acoustic ceiling and look out over the playground. And you can sit and chat on the many stairs and steps in the hall.

Drunk stones

The south wing is covered with acoustic panels. We try to get second-hand, recycled IJssel bricks for the north wall, but the large quantities we need are not available. We discover a round brick kiln that still makes bricks in the traditional way. We buy the duds, the bricks that are scorched and misshapen, and use them for the hundred-metre-long wall. We have to show the masons who normally work in a neat line how to lay the bricks at random. 'Act as if you are drunk', we say. It is important that the wall should be an unforgettable, 'real' wall. The steel construction to support the hall is covered with zinc, and the construction of the gyms is covered with wood. To prevent the volume from seeming too big and top-heavy, it is so designed that it looks as though you can just push the wooden, rounded volume of the gym into the zinc volume of the hall.

Familiar

Sjarel Ex, director of the Centraal Museum in Utrecht, sees the pictures of the Isala College during the Rietveld lecture in 1995. We both attended the Maartens College in Haren, on the southern outskirts of Groningen. The Isala College looks familiar to him. In our mind's eye we walk over the stairs of our old secondary school. We see father Muskens – it is a Jesuit school – standing at a strategic point on the first floor to nod to all the pupils on the stairs. From the classrooms you have a view of the surrounding landscape. We recollect the time when a foal was born in the meadow and that eight hundred school pupils – tongue-tied behind the windows of the classroom – witnessed the event. Sjarel is right, I wanted to evoke the same atmosphere in the Isala College.

95. *West wall with the river landscape and the lane of trees in the foreground*
    Irregular masonry
    East wall with view of gym and main hall
96. *View of the cloakroom in the basement and the hall above it*
97. *Staircase for the pupils*
    First floor with open areas
98. *The corridor as the 'river' of the building*
99. *View of the lane of trees from the entrance hall*
100. *The entrance of the hall*
101. *The main entrance and zinc wall of the hall*
102. *West wall beside the avenue of trees*

The first encounter with the space

In February 1995 Harm van Duin from the theatre company De Trust calls to ask if I would like to convert a church into a theatre. He tells me about the church beside the Kloveniersburgwal in Amsterdam, but he does not tell me the street number. I want to see the building first. We make an appointment to meet and to view the building. I ask one of our staff who lives in Amsterdam to look out for a church beside the Kloveniersburgwal. He tells me next day that he has not been able to find a church. Maybe he was looking for a church with a saddle roof and a clock tower, with its narrow side facing the canal.

Noli me tangere

The first meeting with De Trust and the church terrifies me. The church turns out to be an enormous and austere building in a dilapidated state. It stands proudly with its entire width facing the canal. The interior is an impressive space with double colonnades of Etruscan columns, high windows and a very strong sense of space that emanates unassailability. It is as if the building is shouting at me: 'Don't touch me.' De Trust is an avant-garde theatre company which has been

Church and theatre

playing for years in a theatre that was once a swimming bath. The swimming bath had to make way for a new shopping centre. Theatre companies can be fantastic at improvising, building décors, creating moods. 'Why don't you do it yourselves?' I ask. 'You can do it much better than I can.'

Theatre and church

As Max van Rooy wrote in the article 'Pregnant Playground' in the Trustkrant in September 1995, God, the theatre and the buildings for both of them have been connected with one another almost throughout history. The interiors of the first independent theatres are like the inside of a church. The place in which the audience and the stage face one another is virtually identical to the ground plan of a Roman Catholic church with the main altar where the stage is. Except there are no balconies in the church, because they would raise the faithful above God and his representatives, and that is not the idea. Palladio's son-in-law Scamozzi built a wooden theatre that closely resembles a church in Sabbionetta in 1588. It is the first theatre with technical facilities so that the décors can move and gods and clouds can fly through the air. After the Great Fire of London, the famous English architect Christopher Wren built all the new theatres and churches that London needed, including St Paul's Cathedral. Church or theatre, for the architect Wren it did not matter.

What the organ looked like in this church

Pregnant playground

The church, built in one of the oldest neighbourhoods of Amsterdam, has a turbulent history. It stands on the site of the nunnery of the Eleven Thousand Virgins, which was followed by a mental asylum. In 1792 the Orthodox splinter-group of the Evangelical Lutheran Church purchases the empty Dolhuis, demolishes it, and builds a church there. As the city council has decreed that the premises of churches other than Reformed ones are not allowed to look like churches, the design does not include towers, clocks or striking ornamental decoration. It is a sober, classicist building whose façade hardly betrays the fact that there is a church behind it. The church is built under the supervision of the city architect Abraham van der Hart. During the nineteenth century it is the headquarters from which the Reformists stubbornly try to find their way back to genuine Lutheranism. The rather inflammable character of the church community meant that it was not always quiet in the Kloveniersburgwal: many a real life drama was acted out in the building and out on the street. However, the time-hallowed differences between the different Lutheran sects are ironed out, and in 1952 the Reformists are reunited with the Evangelical Lutherans. They sell the building to De Nederlandse Bank. The interior of the church is demolished and a steel frame is constructed in the empty space on top of a new foundation to store six kilometres of archives. The big organ is donated to the St Eusebius church in Arnhem, whose own organ had been destroyed during the war. The pulpit is moved to the Reformed Church in Elst. The Bank leaves the church in the 1980s, and it stands empty for a few years, waiting for new times.

Organ

The photo of the organ fascinates me. The organ dominates the space, it is decorative, imposing, and makes a church of this sober interior. If it is ever put back here, the building will be a church again. I want to design a Piece of Furniture that will make the space a theatre just as the organ makes it a church. It stands on its own in the empty space and does not touch the colonnade of the old building. The Piece of Furniture changes function on every floor. It serves as a bar, staircase, and kitchen. In the main hall the Piece of Furniture becomes the direction room, and at the highest level it houses the essential installations. Old and new do not come into contact, that is the principle of the details. We do nothing to the old building except what is technically necessary, but the Piece of Furniture must be expressive and decorative. We propose a composition of materials like steel, zinc, copper, brass, glass and painted wood.

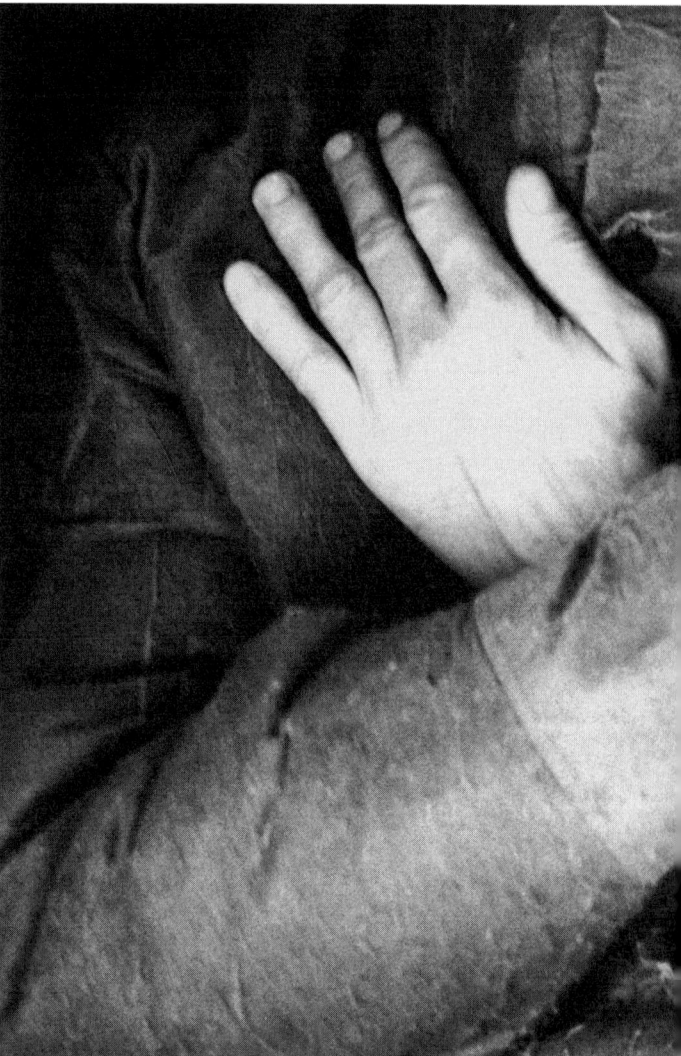

'The Persians' by The Hollandia Dramatic Company

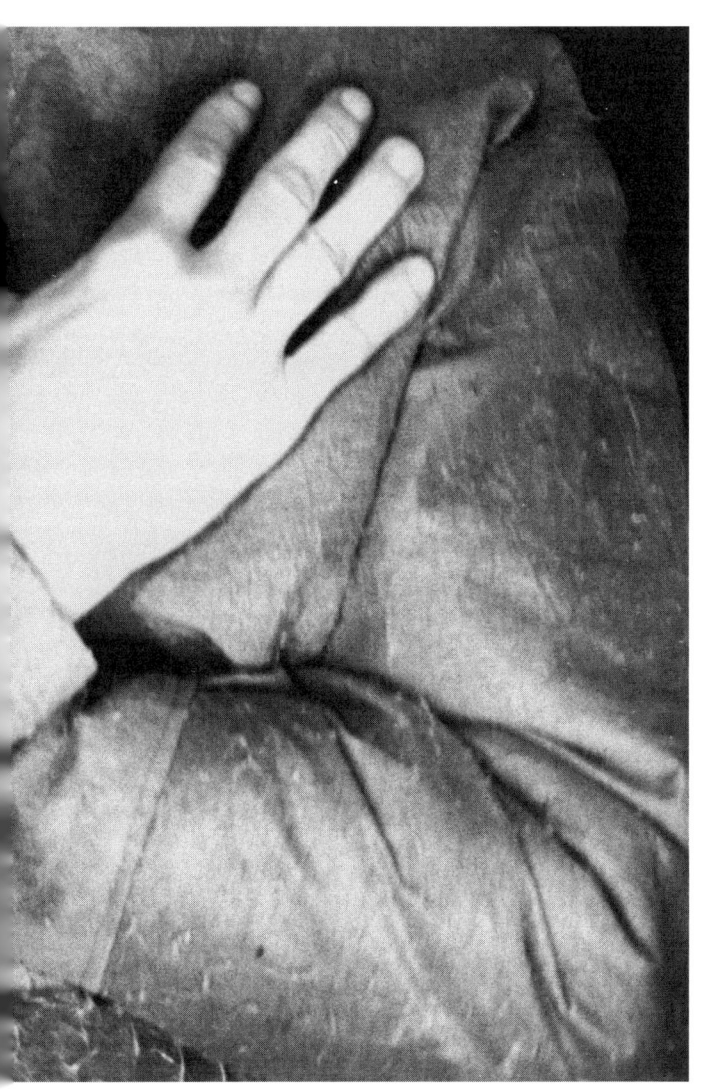

Avant-garde
During the interval between the swimming bath and the church, De Trust plays on the site of the Westergasfabriek in Amsterdam. Under artistic director Theu Boermans the company interprets the tough plays of Werner Schwab and gives a wonderful, sober performance of Chekhov's *Three Sisters*.

As always, avant-garde means broke. Although the minimal amount necessary has not yet been raised, we start on the renovation. It takes some doing, although the interventions are mainly concentrated at the level of the programme and engineering. Apart from the fact that we want to leave the space intact as much as possible, the limited budget does not give us any scope for the luxury of architectural details. No money to paint the walls? Then we leave the outside walls of the church as they are and shine a spotlight on them, so that the weathered plasterwork with the pieces of bare brick seem to become a part of a theatre space. This approach ensures that the church does not disappear behind the theatre. The money to decorate our Piece of Furniture, our 'organ', with an elegant composition turns out to be unavailable too.

Black box
We make the stage on the first floor to create optimal lines of vision and acoustics. This also enables us to create a small theatre, studios and storage space on the ground floor. Five permanent bridges, subtly introduced beneath the vaulted ceiling, are available for the technical fittings. A sliding platform to seat three hundred is placed at a gentle angle so as not to disturb the atmosphere of the space. The stage, in the classic position between the columns, is fourteen metres wide. The colonnades can be used as side stages. But isn't it a nice idea to use the whole level as a stage now and then, with a typical Amsterdam view from the tall windows of the canal, canal houses and the tower of the Zuiderkerk? The black box that is characteristic of every modern theatre is created by closing the deep blue curtains. In the daytime the theatre technicians and actors can enjoy the wonderful lighting that comes into the building. The magic of the black box can be broken by opening a simple curtain.

Candelabra

The actors and actresses help to get the building ready. They sand and paint as if they have no need to rehearse. The foyer chairs are brought from a demolished school in Belgium. The Piece of Furniture is painted blood red on the outside and gold on the inside: the colours of the theatre. Harm van Duin still tries to get me to hang candelabra in the building. I make it clear that I am not opposed to the kitsch look of candelabra, but that I do not like that kind of light. I illuminate the Piece of Furniture with theatre lights. Other lamps are fixed in such a way that they reinforce the idea of keeping the old and the new separate. Finally three candelabra are allowed to be hung inside the Piece of Furniture, where the light is reflected by the golden surface.

Time

Working on this church makes me aware of the time factor. The building is two hundred years old, and may stand there for another two hundred years. I am just a passer-by, a guest. Is that why the protocol in restoring a painting is that you must do it in such a way that your interventions can be reversed? I have come to love this two-hundred-year old building that filled me with dread at first. I embrace and stroke the enormous columns. The building is no longer screaming at me. We work together to make music and theatre. The result is a building in which the pure essence of architecture is achieved by the sense of space, light and mood. And perhaps we will remove the Piece of Furniture in fifty or a hundred years' time and install an organ to turn the building back into a church.

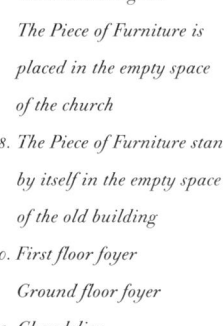

107. *The theatre, Kloveniersburgwal*
     The Piece of Furniture is placed in the empty space of the church
108. *The Piece of Furniture stands by itself in the empty space of the old building*
110. *First floor foyer*
     Ground floor foyer
111. *Chandelier*
112. *Bar and staircase*
113. *The 'black box' is created by closing the dark blue curtains. By day you can enjoy the daylight as it enters the building.*
114. *The theatre with retractable stalls*

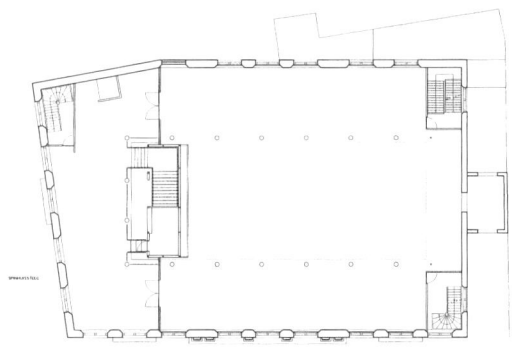

First floor

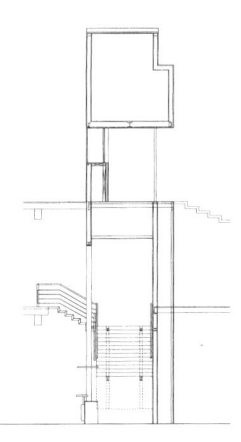 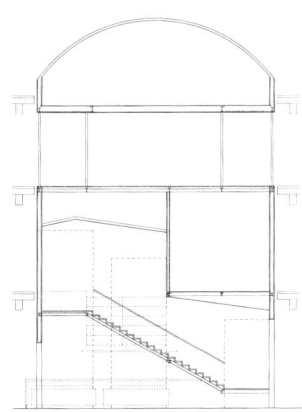

Sections of the Piece of Furniture

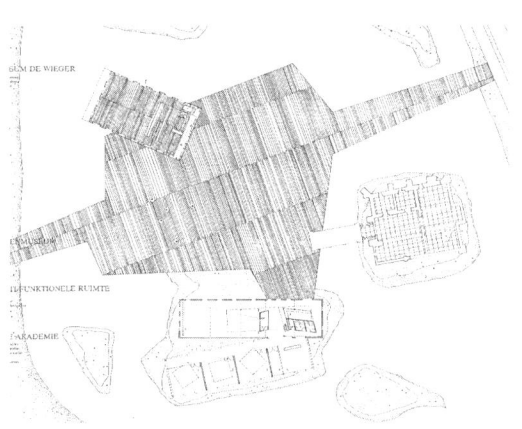
Composition with three buildings in a wooden square

Why do ruins attract people? Why is a dilapidated and run-down building more fascinating than the original building? Ruins have featured in literature as a décor over the centuries: as a place to meditate, to compose, to sing, to mourn destruction and transience, to carry on living with an egoistic satisfaction.

In the heyday of Romanticism fantasy ruins were an important part of park design. They are a nostalgic memory of bygone times and cultures. They make you realise that nature wins in the end. Nature overruns decaying cathedrals and monasteries and even sends cities to the bottom of the sea. Decay, a visible passage of time, makes you aware that people only have a marginal influence. In the Italian Renaissance gardens and in the English landscape parks they made new ruins, where genuine ones were lacking, as a non-functional element in a carefully arranged décor. The mystery of decay and the tangible presence of time and nature fill the viewer with respect.

The ruin of beauty

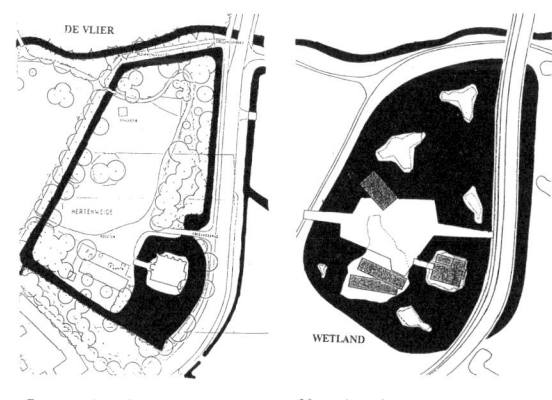
Present situation   *New situation*

In Western society we only allow a few buildings to turn into ruins. What is no longer functional usually disappears silently to make place for a new building. What is left are drawings, photographs and memories. A ruin that is reconstructed and adapted to the present day loses the patina of the past and transience. Time goes on and must be respected as an autonomous being. The ruin of beauty is more beautiful than beauty itself.

Deurne

The Great or New Castle is situated in the Peel. It was built in the fifteenth century by the Deurne family. Next to the castle stands the Dinghuis, which has been in use as the town hall and courthouse since the seventeenth century. Most of the castle was destroyed by fire during bombardment by the Allies in 1944. An investigation into the possible locations for the local De Wieger Museum in 1994 suggested the castle as one of the alternatives. After the castle has been left in ruins for almost half a century, the local authority issues a multiple commission to give the castle and the park surrounding it a central function within the cultural life of Deurne. A programme of requirements includes a Museum, a Free Academy and a Nature and Environment Education Centre.

During my first visit to the location I see the ruins of the Great Castle and the Dinghuis. They are situated in a remarkable setting, on the edge of the marshy landscape of the Peel. The same day I visit the National Park De Groote Peel, a beautiful park that reveals the history of this landscape and what was originally a very poor region. I decide to make a plan that is about not only the historical context of a single building but also about the landscape surrounding it.

Peel

The name Peel comes from the Latin locus paludosus, marshy place. In the course of a process that lasted millions of years, cracks in the earth's surface created a layer that is impenetrable by water. A marshy, impassable region was gradually created above it, characterised by extreme quiet and spaciousness. It had a dangerous reputation and for centuries it was a haven for hermits and people on the run. It is not by coincidence that the border between two provinces, formerly two countries, runs right through the middle of the Peel marshes. Different groups of people lived on each side, each with their own language and customs.

In the Middle Ages small pieces of swamp at the edge were brought under cultivation or cut for turf. There are only a few points where it is possible to cross the swamp. One of the possibilities was the road via Deurne to the east. This strategic point for access to the Peel marshes expanded to become a centre of power in the first half of the nineteenth century. Two fortified villas were built, the Great Castle and the Small Castle. A barrier was erected to exact a toll, which was still in operation after the Second World War.

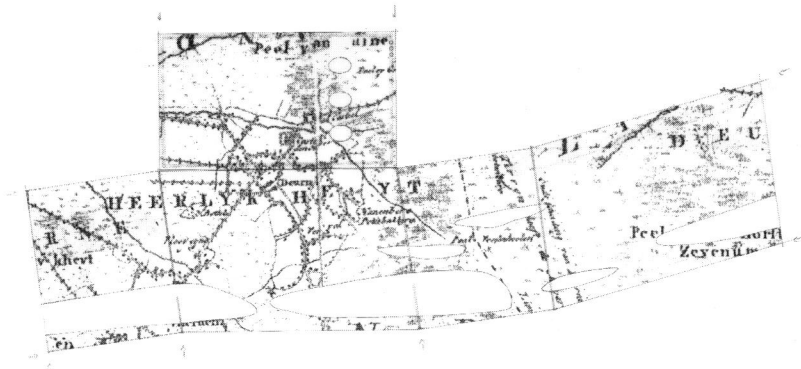
Metal wall engraved with the map of the Deurne seigneury from 1850

Composition

We do not give the ruins a practical function. This is to reinforce their architectural strength and cultural significance. The ruins serve as a frame of reference, as a décor for the arts, as an annual outdoor exhibition by the De Wieger Museum, to inspire artists and to challenge them to react. We leave the ruins as ruins.

The outside of the Dinghuis is restored. On the inside the old walls and the roof construction are made visible. The new multifunctional hall is incorporated in this carcass. This new hall acquires an identity of its own through the contrast with the old shell. At a future stage an extension can be carried out behind the Dinghuis to accommodate the Free Academy.

The De Wieger Museum is a new, contemporary building: a sculptural volume, encased in a metal outer wall, in which the map of the Deurne seigneury from 1850 is engraved. You take the lift up to the top floor of the museum and walk through the various rooms and cabinets. Each room has different natural lighting and a different orientation. Windows and views can be introduced in the metal outer wall to suit one's needs. The basement houses the workshop and store. These three buildings, each with its own language, expression and biography, form a joint composition in a wooden square.

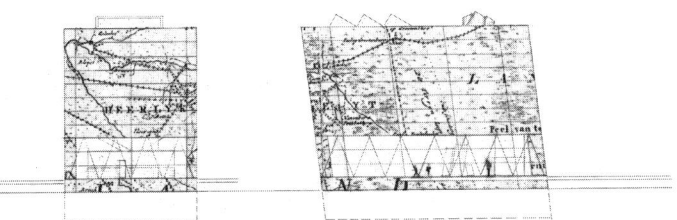
Walls of the museum

119 - 122. Scale model of the cultural complex in a wetland

Wetlands

We set the whole cultural complex in a wetland, a shallow lake with wild grass, moss and a few islands. It is an extension of the moat of the Great Castle. It also conveys the impression of the old landscape of the Peel and is thus an extra support for the Nature and Environment Education Centre that is to be set up there and for the surrounding region. Skating on it in the winter is a delightful prospect. The wooden square is a reference to the wooden bridges and paths that were made through the marshes. It functions as a plateau that links the various parts of the programme of the cultural centre together.

Nature is part of the architecture in the design. The idea is to create a unique cultural centre specially for this single location, based on its own history and that of the surrounding countryside.

Beauty of contrast

During the presentation of the plan I talk to the jury about a carefully placed composition of three buildings on a plateau. Wim Quist, who is a member of the jury, asks me whether there are rules for my compositions. I tell him that I can only explain that in terms of a Japanese cookery book called *A feast for your eyes*. It is about serving and arranging a Japanese meal. The book explains that a regular, symmetrical pattern is dull because there is nothing exciting about it. Space, or rather emptiness, is an essential part of the composition. If you are dealing with three elements, you must avoid placing them at the same distance from one another. Arrange them as a main element, a subsidiary element and a subordinate element: the resulting composition has a nice rhythm and a certain elegance.

It is fantastic to be able to design different types of libraries. We designed a faculty library for the University of Wageningen, and a public library for the city of Almelo. Our third library is to be the central library of Delft Technical University, the technical library of the Netherlands, linked by the latest electronic devices to libraries all over the world.

Books

Of course we discuss the modern electronic media and the question of whether books and libraries still have a future. After all, eventually all information will be available at all times and in all places, from the tiniest student room to the biggest lab. A university library, however, also offers space for knowledge and research, calm and reflection. It is a meeting place where ideas are exchanged. The programme covers a thousand study places. That means that warmth and light will be given to more than three thousand students a day.

I dream of a building with books, books and more books, and with beautiful round reading rooms. A building where you can see, feel and smell books. The gap between dream and reality is large. According to the programme of requirements,

Library of the future

all the books will be kept in store. You only receive a book in your hands after requesting it by computer. The bookless library seems close at hand.

Romanticism

I am from Delft. I studied there, and our firm is based there. I came to Delft more than twenty years ago. I cycled through the wind and the rain to the very last building in the Mekelweg, the Architecture building. Students complained a lot about the Technical University campus. It is too windy, it has a cold atmosphere, the buildings are too modern and there are only a few female students. The buildings aren't all that bad, I think. 'Just wait', the lecturers say. 'Wait until the trees have grown. Then it will be something.'

Twenty years later we have been invited to submit a design for the library. I often go to the location and have come to see it differently by now. Yes, the trees have grown. In fact, the elms have grown so fast that the Mekelweg itself looks like a huge building. But nothing has fundamentally changed in the neighbourhood in those twenty years. The contrast between the tall trees and the bare, concrete area around the aula is enormous. I want to introduce Romanticism into the Technical University area. I dream of rolling lawns, solitary trees, blossom, diagonal paths. I want a campus with old and new buildings, a place where you can stop studying for a while and enjoy sitting outside. The aula and the new library must form the heart, they must come to be situated in a park-like landscape.

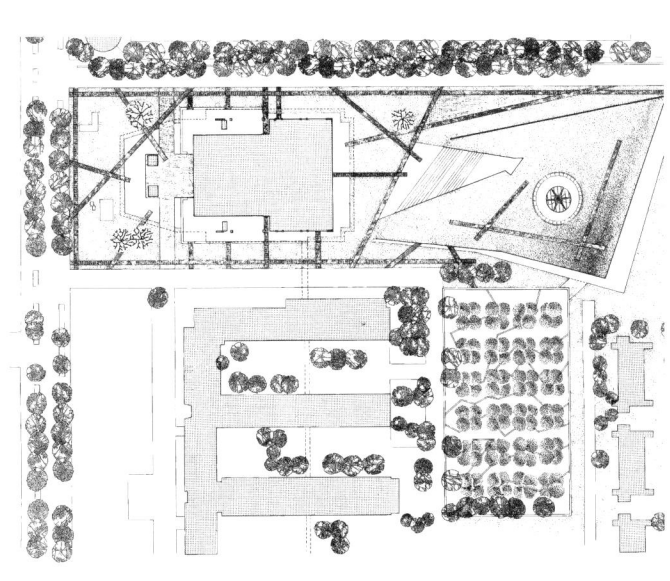

Frog
The faculty buildings in the Mekelweg stand to attention, they do not converse with one another. They stare ahead and just stand there. The aula by Van den Broek and Bakema breaks up the strict axis of the Mekelweg. This interruption emphasises the prominent position of the building. The aula is different. The aula has something fascinating. Is it beautiful or ugly? In the end I come to love the building, but the sense of unassailability remains: the aula does not tolerate any other building beside it. It looks like a spaceship that has descended on an unearthly Mars. It is a rude concrete building on a concrete surface. The shape of the building resembles a frog. And the frog needs grass.

Terminal
The programme of requirements for the new library building places a lot of emphasis on the regulation of flows of information by means of the electronic media. Librarian Leo Waaijers imagines the efficiency of an airport terminal. With the Dutch example of Schiphol airport in mind, you can imagine something positive as far as the handling of passages and flows of goods is concerned. Schiphol is beautiful, but in terms of image and mood it is not suitable as a library. If I think of an attractive passenger terminal that could have some connection with the atmosphere of a library, it is the Saarinen TWA terminal in New York, with a wonderful organic roof and a spacious hall beneath.

Grass and glass
The library is a building that does not really want to be a building, but a landscape. We place the frog on a big lawn and then we raise the lawn on one side like a sheet of paper, place columns beneath it, and fill the walls with glass: a building of grass and glass. It has to remain a landscape, with gently curving shapes; only the ends may be sharp. You must be able to walk literally over the library.

Cone
A large volume is called for to contrast with the landscape. For a long time we think about the precise form. It should be round, but we have our doubts about how the volume should end. In the end the logic of construction determines the shape: a cone, like a tepee on the landscape. The nice thing about the cone is its pure, constructive form as a symbol of the Technical University. The cone gives shape to the round, introverted reading rooms. They hang from the apex of the cone, giving the hall a large space free of columns. The cone as a symbol of technology, but also of calm and contemplation. Like a drawing pin, it pins down the 'endless form of the landscape'.

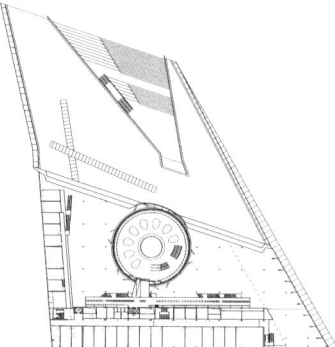
First floor

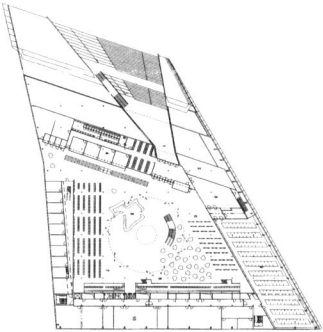
Ground floor

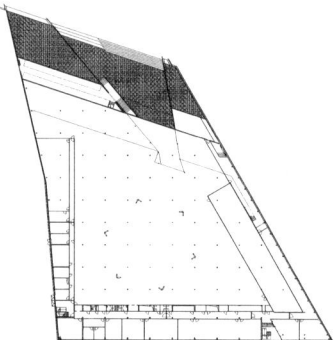
Basement

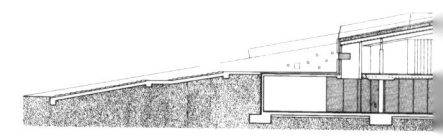
Section

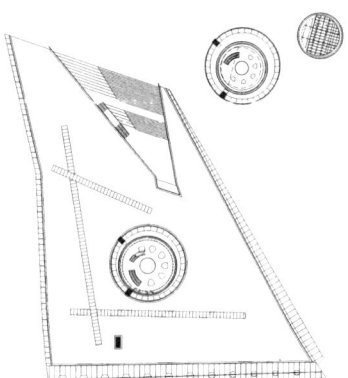
Third and fourth floor

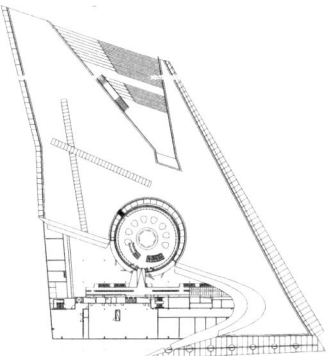
Second floor

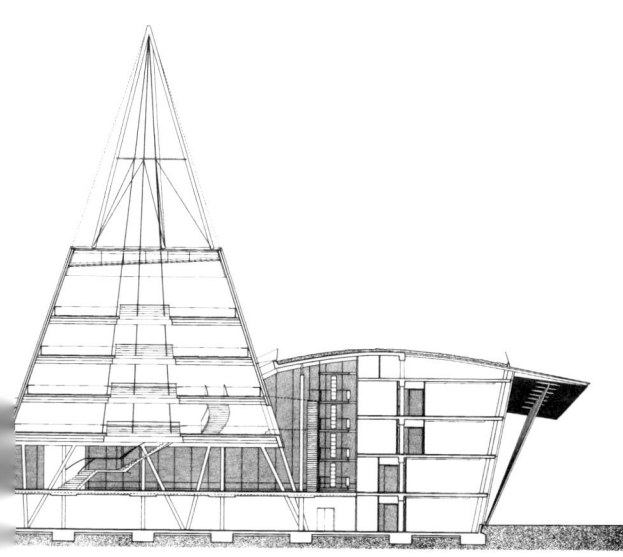

Treasure chamber
Before you go in, you can take a look in the depot. You enter by walking over the books. The glass book lift connects with the enormous depot, that is surrounded by offices, work stations and study areas, with a glass wall sunk into the grass. Behind this glass wall and the room with the study areas a red wall marks the presence of the treasure chamber with the rare books: the crown jewels. The climate of the treasure chamber satisfies the most stringent demands.

Light and warmth
Space, light and relaxing acoustics are lasting values for the design of a library. You must automatically fall silent when you enter it, like a cathedral. The library is open in the daytime and at night. The building literally radiates light and warmth. At night the interior becomes exterior: the blue and red wall can be seen from outside. The car park suddenly turns out to be gaily illuminated.

You can also feel the landscape inside. The metal ceiling runs through all the rooms without interruption and is gently lit from the columns. The columns support, illuminate and heat the hall. The enormous, extended floor has been given the colour of the Sahara. The blue wall with the hanging bookcase is almost a décor: you cannot mistake the fact that it is a library. The blue is the electric blue of the theatre. It makes the bookcase float even more than it actually does.

Order of battle
The work station room is filled with three hundred computers. Computers often dominate the view in a chaotic fashion. The examples we know are not very encouraging. As in the old Bibliothèque Nationale in Paris, the study places are at long tables. We add partitions for privacy, to shade the light from the computer monitor, and as a way of ordering the space. Like a Mondrian composition, we make a pattern of red place-mats on the tables, an allusion to the leather inlay in the tables of old libraries. The books, periodicals and computers are drawn up in a good order of battle. The large desk is the hub of the library. This is where you can obtain information, where searching is done, and where books are lent and returned. The glass lift sends the books up from the enormous depot. The desk has an organic shape, like a fragment of bark from Caucasian Zelkova.

Eco, grass and trees

The building has a carefully thought out eco-technology: the grass roof, the climate wall, the cold and heat storage, and the depot sunk into the ground, where the books are kept like a good wine. As an architect you are used to choosing materials – often you select from hundreds of types of bricks – but it is an experience to be able to select the right type of grass some day. There turn out to be hundreds of types of grass. When the concrete paving stones around the Van den Broek and Bakema aula are removed, the turf is unrolled. Never before have so many strips of turf been unrolled at the same time in the Netherlands. The aula seems to float! We have got two new buildings: the library supports the landscape, and the aula has descended on the landscape.

For the solitary trees that are given a place in this landscape we choose two bog oaks, three beeches and a false honey-locust. The car park, designed like a painting, is decorated with flowering black cherry trees. They fit marvellously into the composition of the new black stones separated by white lines and the recycled stones from the old car park.

Symbiosis

The university expects the arrival of the library to create a demand for extra capacity in the university restaurant to the rear of the aula, so during the building of the library TU Vastgoed asks us to expand the aula. I cannot change this young monument, for me a sacrosanct concrete sculpture, in this way. I go back to the client with the proposal to give me the budget for the expansion and to let me use it to alter the interior of the restaurant in order to solve the problem of capacity. They agree. Slowly we creep into the skin of the frog and renew its organs one by one without killing it. We renew the restaurant, make a bar, and place a few counters and a new lift in the hall. All with respect for Van den Broek and Bakema.

In the end the view from the university restaurant is one of my favourite spots from which to look at the landscape of the library. Frog and library, complete symbiosis.

---

127. Library entrance with hall in foreground
128. East wing with offices
129. Library entrance North wall: a building of grass and glass
130. Entrance cone from the bookcase Hanging bookcase
131. Cone in situ
132. Blue wall with 80,000 books
133. Study room in cone Work site room with 300 computers
134. Hall seen from the library Library seen from the hall

Railway embankments, storage depots, warehouses and factories – fascinating places, especially if they have just been abandoned. You can drift off into dreams there: the buildings tell stories. You can fantasize there: which dream can I make true here? Every city has locations like these, which gradually yield their secrets when their original economic function has disappeared. There is often an environmental problem. The Westergasfabriek in Amsterdam, a former gas processing plant, is a location of this kind, situated on the outskirts of the city, and yet right in the middle at the same time. The fifteen hectare site has contaminated soil, twenty-two very diverse buildings, and a strong magnetic power.

I know the Westergasfabriek site because the theatre company De Trust had its office there temporarily in 1996 while the new Trusttheater was being built in the Kloveniersburgwal. We often hold meetings in the attic of the Purifying Building. Theatre companies like Toneelgroep Amsterdam, De Trust, The Hollandia Dramatic Company and Orkater regularly perform on the site, and exhibitions, fashion shows and music festivals are held there too. One time the gas holder is the location for a large-scale opera, the next weekend it is the setting for an enormous house party.

Aerial view of Westergasfabriek, 1997

Changement

The site is the new décor for cultural Amsterdam. It is part of a long, green zone running from east to west starting with the romantic nineteenth-century Westerpark, then the gas processing site, which gradually passes via allotments and a polder landscape into nature reserves. The zone is bounded by the Haarlemmervaart and the railway.

Foreign landscape architect

The Franco-American landscape architect Kathryn Gustafson sent me a fax in 1997 to ask whether I wanted to make a joint submission with her to the closed international competition for the Park of the Future. I was very tempted and curious to work with a foreign landscape architect, with someone who thinks about landscape from a different cultural background. A month later we walked through the location together and the first ideas were born. She spoke in sculptural language about moving and raising the ground as if it is clay, about visual axes and perspectives, about making fountains. I argued for the need to make a large lawn, like Regents Park in London and the big meadow in Central Park in New York, where you can picnic, read, laze around, and sometimes enjoy a wonderful concert. We made sketches on the spot. The end of the park needed a building volume. I flew one more time to Paris for a final discussion in Kathryn's studio. The finishing touch was made to our submission in the Delft office. We won!

Path of dreams

A new, clear structure places the monumental buildings in a new context. A long axis connects the different areas of the park, while the diagonal 'path of dreams' prevents the axis from becoming too compulsive. The two routes lead you past the Westerpark, the floral bed, the wood, the field for events, the village, the orchard, the waterfront, the Cité des Arts, the water and nature garden, and finally the nature reserve. You can experience large spaces and distant views on an area of fifteen hectares. There is both a connection and a contrast with the surrounding city districts, the Westerpark and the polder. The Cité des Arts is a new complex that is neither building nor landscape: walls of wood, grass and vegetation form patios and outdoor studios.

Veil of sound and water

In the daytime the big lawn is the heart of the park where sport, play and events take place. The wind plays with a veil of sound and water in a pond on the northern side of the lawn. You can sit on the slope, which works like a natural auditorium during open air performances. The park is a neighbourhood park and a city park at the same time. There is space for culture and nature. The park is not static or rigid, but it can assume different guises. Just as a performance can change the mood in the theatre, so the park must be able to change colour and offer scope for a continuously changing range of programmes, events and performances.

Supervisor

Kathryn and Neil Porter direct the design and implementation of the park from their London office. Evert Verhagen, project director of the Westergasfabriek, asks me to act as supervisor and to make a master plan for all the buildings on the site in order to bring about an ideal coherence between the park and the buildings. The Westergasfabriek is a challenge, the cultural world is a source of inspiration. Fantastic activities are already going on there under the direction of Liesbeth Janssen. The buildings have been temporarily rented out to organisations in the field of theatre, film and music. It takes a lot of care to preserve the uniqueness of the location. Trying to find what matches it in terms of function and architecture is a complex task.

Sketch for park design

Eclectic style

We get absorbed in the buildings and their history. The plant was in operation from 1883 to 1967. Most of the buildings were designed by Isaac Gosschalk in an eclectic style known as Dutch Renaissance. They are built with bricks, and the outer walls are designed and worked out in detail, with citations of styles here and there from architecture. They are attractive industrial buildings with unusual steel roof structures. There are also a number of round gas holders and houses for the overseers. After the factory ceased operations, a number of the buildings and gas holders were demolished and local authority departments moved into the remaining premises. The site was abandoned in 1992 and the local authority decided that the future function of the buildings would be for cultural activities. Thirteen of the twenty-two buildings are on the list of historic monuments. The buildings stand sternly to attention and reflect the industrial process. Through their different shapes they can accommodate a large variety of activities.

Villages

Directors of theatre companies like to perform in old industrial buildings because of the unusual natural lighting and the patina. However, the buildings do not satisfy technical and acoustic criteria, and there are no sanitary facilities. This means that you have to construct everything anew for each performance or event. This is inconvenient and costs a lot of energy and money. So as not to lose the patina, we decide to let the buildings speak for themselves and to apply a programme that leaves the value of the building intact. We introduce villages, each with its own atmosphere, programme and noise level. The Spectacle Village, the Village, the Kids Village, the Cité des Arts, and the Westerpark. The Spectacle Village is equipped for large-scale events with the gas holder as the main attraction. The Village acquires the intimacy of a theatre village with workshops for the cultural companies, halls, studios and a cinema. The Mobile Foyer ensures that the original purifying rooms can be used in a variety of ways. The Kids Village is the place where children can go after school. The surrounding gardens are to play in. Cité des Arts becomes the location for small studios with patio-like inner gardens. The workshop buildings and the engineering buildings are incorporated in the atmosphere of the Westerpark. So you can imagine that we let ivy grow over it like a country house in Scotland and turn it into an attractive hotel. The villages make it possible for the architecture of each area of the site to have a character of its own.

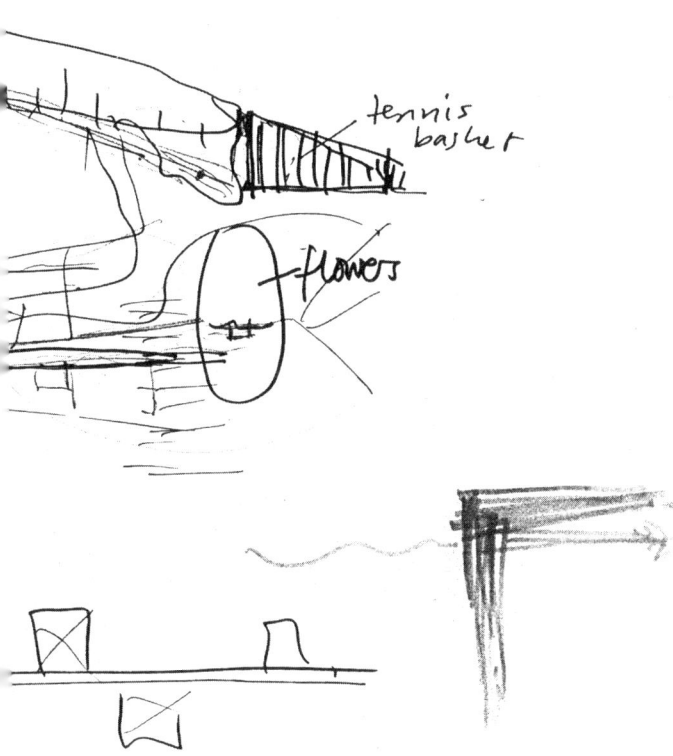

The gas holder in 1903

139. Processing plant
    Interior processing plant
    The gas holder in 1997
    Processing plant used for
    fashion show
    Performance in the gas holder
140. Change of building volume
    and of season in the
    Cité des Arts
141. Master plan
142. Sketches of gas holder and
    processing plant

Gas holder

We refer to this as the gas holder, but it is only the lower part of what was the biggest gas holder in the Netherlands when it was constructed in 1903. The actual gas holder with a capacity of 10,000 m³ has been demolished. The gigantic cylinder with a cross-section and height of sixty metres looks impressive in the photographs. Dual use of the land was decided on in 1883 because the site was too small for shunting. The space below the gas holder was used as a storage area and as a turning-point for trains. A spidery metal construction keeps this impressive space, which is 13.5 metres tall and has a floating roof spanning sixty metres, entirely free of columns. Another space that radiates unassailability!

By using a large object – a cloud, a fish, a submarine – hanging in the steel tentacles of a new structure, we want to make the gas holder the symbol of the change from a gas processing plant to a site of cultural production. We carry on trying to find the right programme and form with the project developer that has by now been selected for the buildings, the MAB from The Hague. They ask us to act as the architect for the whole site. We continue our search in a new role each time: from landscape architect to supervisor to architect.

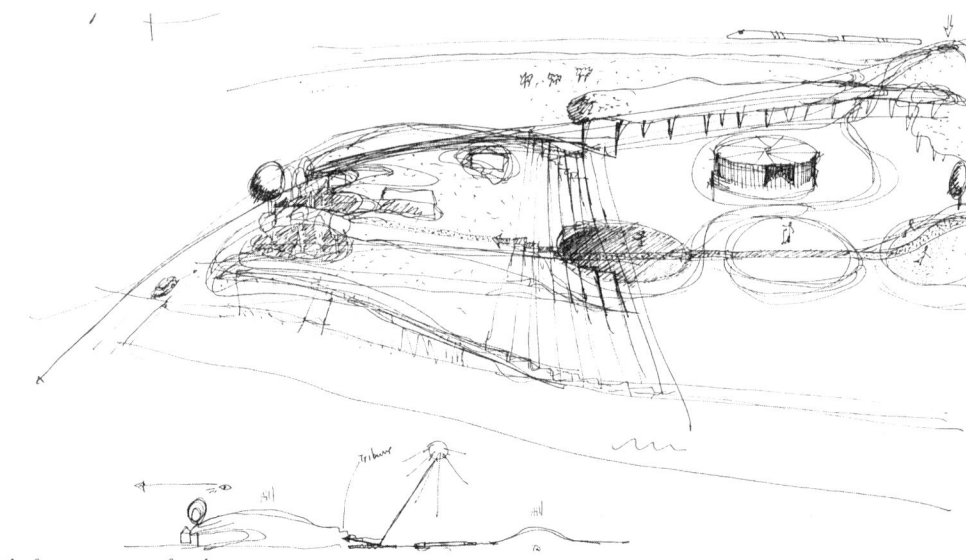

Sketch of western corner of park

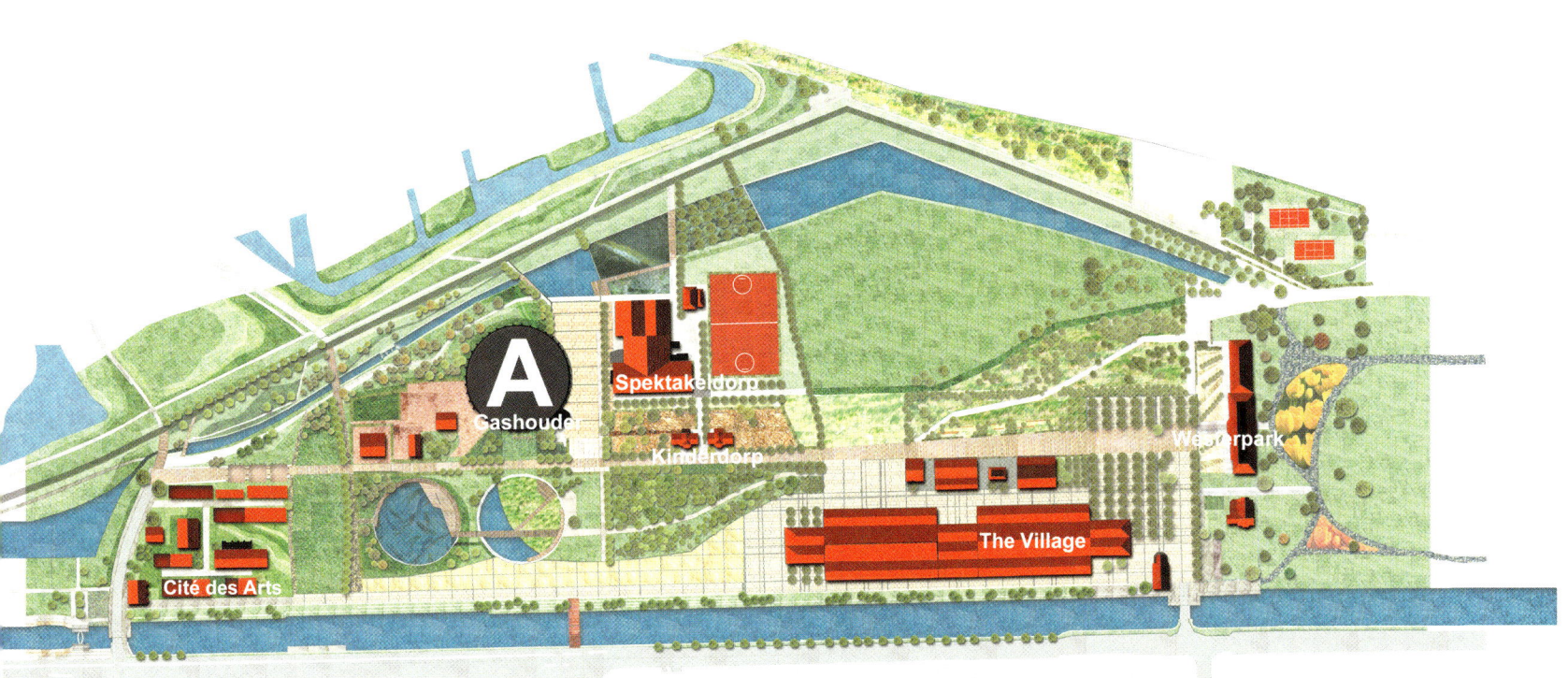

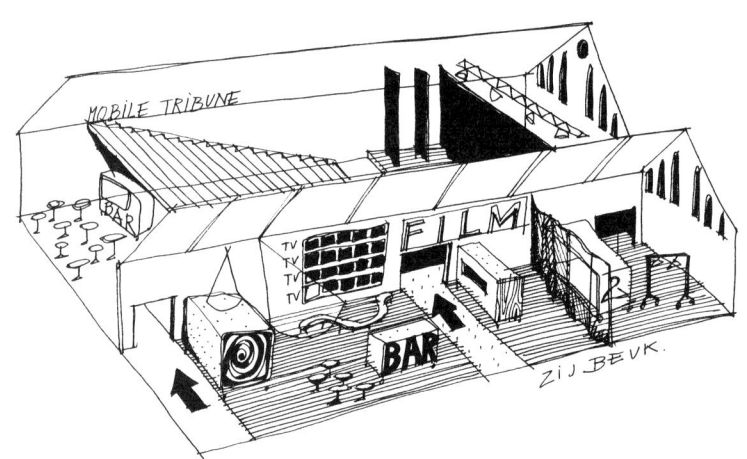

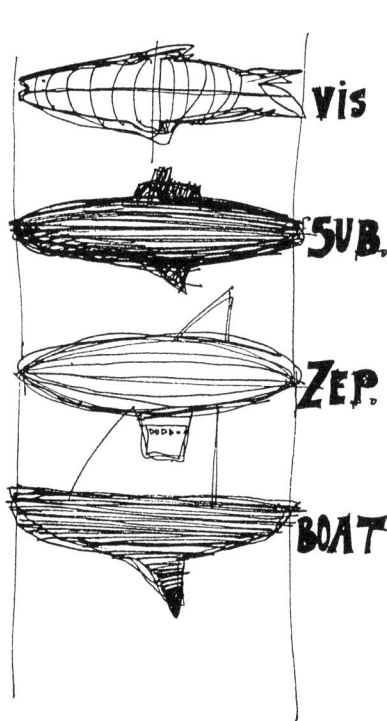

We are good at creating new land in the Netherlands, we have been doing it for centuries. The pride of Holland is called the polder. The polders are the Dutch works of art, but they are inconspicuous. It is flat land with a dyke around it. First bare like a windy desert, later as fertile as an oasis. The New Land is land without visible history, land at the bottom of the Zuyderzee, a horizon with Dutch skies. That is the task facing you as a designer: you have to think up a town. We are good at creating new land, but creating a new town is something very different. A town is never complete, and the perfect town does not exist. It is unnatural to make a town too quickly. A town has to take root too.

Expedition, 1996

In 1996 we are asked by Riek Bakker to think about what the town of Almere ought to look like in the year 2015. Almere is sit-

Eco town, nature town, water town

uated in Flevoland, the twelfth and youngest Dutch province. It consists of three polders in a drained sea bed with a total of 140,000 hectares. It is new, flat land with agricultural areas, nature reserves, towns and villages. Between 20,000 and 30,000 houses will be built in Almere before 2015, which entails a population growth of around 100,000. A spatial development strategy is therefore called for.
I go in search of the assignment. I do not just want to sketch districts, streets and housing typologies, but I want to know what it means to design a town. Resolutely I try to find what I am looking for, without knowing what my goal is.

Bus lane, 1974

In 1974, my first year as a student, the design principles of new towns like Almere were regularly explained in the lectures.
I was not particularly struck by them. They seemed to be a way of designing that concentrates above all on the public transport system by bus. For me Almere is a drawing with a circular thick black line (bus lane) with a black dot (bus stop) every 400 metres. It is surrounded by a thin black circle, with the same 400 metres, which indicates the area where the residential districts are situated. We go on an excursion to Almere when another experiment is being constructed. As we cannot find the way by car, we sneak into the prohibited bus lane.

Dertienhuizen

Dertienhuizen, 1990

In 1990 we design the Dertienhuizen project for the first trade fair for the building profession, the BouwRai. We and the client note that the population of Almere no longer consists of just average new town residents: the ideal family with a father, a mother and two children. Almere is acquiring the same mixed population as the 'old towns'. We design a residence in the polder. A house with an architecture that matches the polder town of Almere and that, like the canal houses in Amsterdam, can stand up to many changes in society. We even develop a special, low bike shed as a protest against the omnipresent, dominant bike sheds in new housing estates.

Veertienhuizen

Veertienhuizen, 1992

Two years later, in 1992, we design the Veertienhuizen project for the second BouwRai. These are houses with optimal user flexibility and even the opportunity to expand. The accent this time is on unusual divisions of land as an alternative to the average divisions into streets, rows of houses and bike sheds. Inspired by the houses that Jan Wils designed in 1920 in the Papaverhof in The Hague, we design staggered back to back houses. Experimental houses are often constructed for exhibitions. You reach a large audience and it is an attempt to promote the discussion of architecture and then to apply it on a large scale. This is not what happens in Almere. Experiments are only for clearly demarcated incidents like building exhibitions, while the town – with a building production of 3,000 houses a year – continues to grow.

Almere 2015, 1996

In 1996 I jettison all my prejudices about Almere and try to understand the town in a few weekends. It is an extended area of sixteen by sixteen kilometres. I want to start out from my own impressions and sketch what I do and do not like, or rather, what surprises me. For instance, I cannot understand why you do not build the town beside the water if you are surrounded by fantastic water. The famous bus lane seems to function smoothly, but this asphalt lane, which is only accessible for the bus and goes past the backs of the houses, is still ugly to me. I fly in a Cesna over the whole area. From the air Almere looks like a big model. Even the regularly placed trees look like balls on a stick. You can recognise all the influences and styles of city planning from the Seventies, Eighties and Nineties: from small-scale and cosy to austere with big lines.

As a preliminary exercise we project 20,000 houses over thirty different potential building locations in the present town. But that is looking too far ahead. Perhaps in fifty years' time.

New town, old town

A new town is always grappling with time. The new town wants to look older than it really is. New towns try to approach the intimacy and identity of an old town. Almere tries to do that in 1971 by imitating the canals of Delft. But it turns out not to be as simple as that. The feeling of an old town is much more complex and is not just the product of a form of urban planning. In 1996 Almere is twenty-five years old and it is the size of the trees that gives me the impression that the town has grown up. I conclude that Almere must derive her identity primarily from the (malleable) landscape. I want to combine that identity with my attempt to design a sustainable town, an eco town.

Red, yellow, purple, blue and green

Wherever I am abroad, there is always a book about the city in the hotel room. A book that has usually been compiled under the auspices of the local Chamber of Commerce and that also presents the future plans of the city to tempt potential investors. No matter whether it is Rome, Madrid, Los Angeles or São Paulo, the development of the city is illustrated on a map with red, purple, yellow, blue and green: housing, industrial areas, roads, water and greenery. That is apparently how cities are planned. The maps do not express any identity at all. I make the maps of Almere more intuitively. Can a map be tactile too, can it convey an atmosphere and an identity? Can a map express how I want to see the relation between town and countryside? I make a map about the position of Almere with respect to Amsterdam, the Green Heart, the Oostvaardersplassen, and the towns in the Gooi. This map expresses the fact that Almere can no longer be regarded as a satellite of Amsterdam, but as a town that belongs to the towns of the Gooi countryside.

Town on the Gooi Lake

Almere becomes the town of the Gooi Lake. Unlike traditional towns, the heart of the town is 'empty': the Weerwater and the Waterlandse Bos. Almere becomes the town with a lot of nature and landscape, where recreation on a large scale is possible in the immediate surroundings. In terms of housing environment, Almere fits in with the Gooi. Through an extension of the rail network and expansion of the motorways via the Hollandse Brug and the Stichtse Brug, Almere can be made accessible from Amsterdam, the Gooi towns and the rest of the Netherlands. The town receives two new economic impulses. The Center for Environmental Design, that is situated on a large and broad eco viaduct over the A6 motorway, near the intersection with the A27, where the links with every part of the Netherlands meet. A town for living and working is created near the Stichtse Brug, a new sort of business centre in which the distinction between housing and commercial or industrial buildings disappears and that has the flexibility to be able to adapt to social developments in the future.

Strategy Gooistad Almere 2005-2015

Residential areas in the countryside

The existing centre is upgraded and orientated towards the enlarged Weerwater. The centre of Almere-Haven is reconstructed and turned into a genuine harbour town with allure. The four centres – Harbour, Town, Center for Environmental Design, and the Stichtse Brug – are connected with one another by high-quality public transport. These four cores are separated by residential areas situated in the countryside with as little asphalt as possible. These residential areas, combined with the abundant supply of water, the nature and the recreational facilities, determine the identity of Almere as a nature town, sport town, recreation town, water town and bike town. These additions, combined with a number of interventions in the existing town, make Almere a town with more contrast, a town with clear centres, with high-quality facilities and employment, combined with residential areas in the countryside. The new elements are attuned to a more mixed composition of the population. We formulate clearly where we do not want to build, and where we do want to build, it is done in a manner that is appropriate to the landscape.

Strategy of haste, 1997

The 1996 study was very inspiring. There is a great distance, however, separating dream from reality. Every time there is the haste. In 1997 Almere asks us to develop a housing typology for a large district on the outskirts of the large nature reserve, the Oostvaardersplassen. It is a project involving 7,000 houses, most of them single family homes, with their parking lot on their own land. The idea behind this is that the costs of parking lots are then borne by the individual resident rather than by the budget of the local authority.

As a result of the enormous pressure of time, decay has set in at the level of urban planning. Housing (red) and work (purple) are being completely separated from one another. In one of the most attractive locations in the plan area, directly adjacent to the Oostvaardersplassen, an industrial estate has been planned. Sports fields are planned in the remote corners of the town without any link with the residential areas. We propose varied districts with character and let the proximity of the Oostvaardersplassen make its presence felt. Sport, water and recreation are the pillars of the plan. We apply the ideas of the BouwRai exhibitions on a large scale and make an urban plan entitled 'Strategy of haste'.

Green River

In order to gain a lot of time in the first stage, we repeat a number of successful districts which have recently been implemented. We still have the working drawings of these plans in the cupboard. The time we save is used to design and develop the next stages. This gives the client and the architect the time to think up specific districts. We want to develop a home and work district here. We place houseboats in a number of large canals. We allocate between 10 and 20% of the area as concession land. This is land that is exempt from the Building Decree, where all kinds of experiments can be carried out, such as communes, mobile homes, monasteries/nunneries, home and work villas, and settlements. The Green River winds through the plan, an elongated, winding park ending in the Oostvaardersplassen. It is a plan with contrasts in density, housing typologies and public space. It is intended as a guideline and as a strategy for a potentially wonderful town next to a large-scale Dutch nature reserve: the Oostvaardersplassen.

147. Almere in relation to Amsterdam, the Gooi and the Green Heart Map Almere 2015
148. Fragments and images Eco town, Nature town, Water town
150. Strategy of haste

Bird's-eye view of Almere

CENTRE FOR ENVIRONMENTAL DESIGN

OVERGOOISE VELD

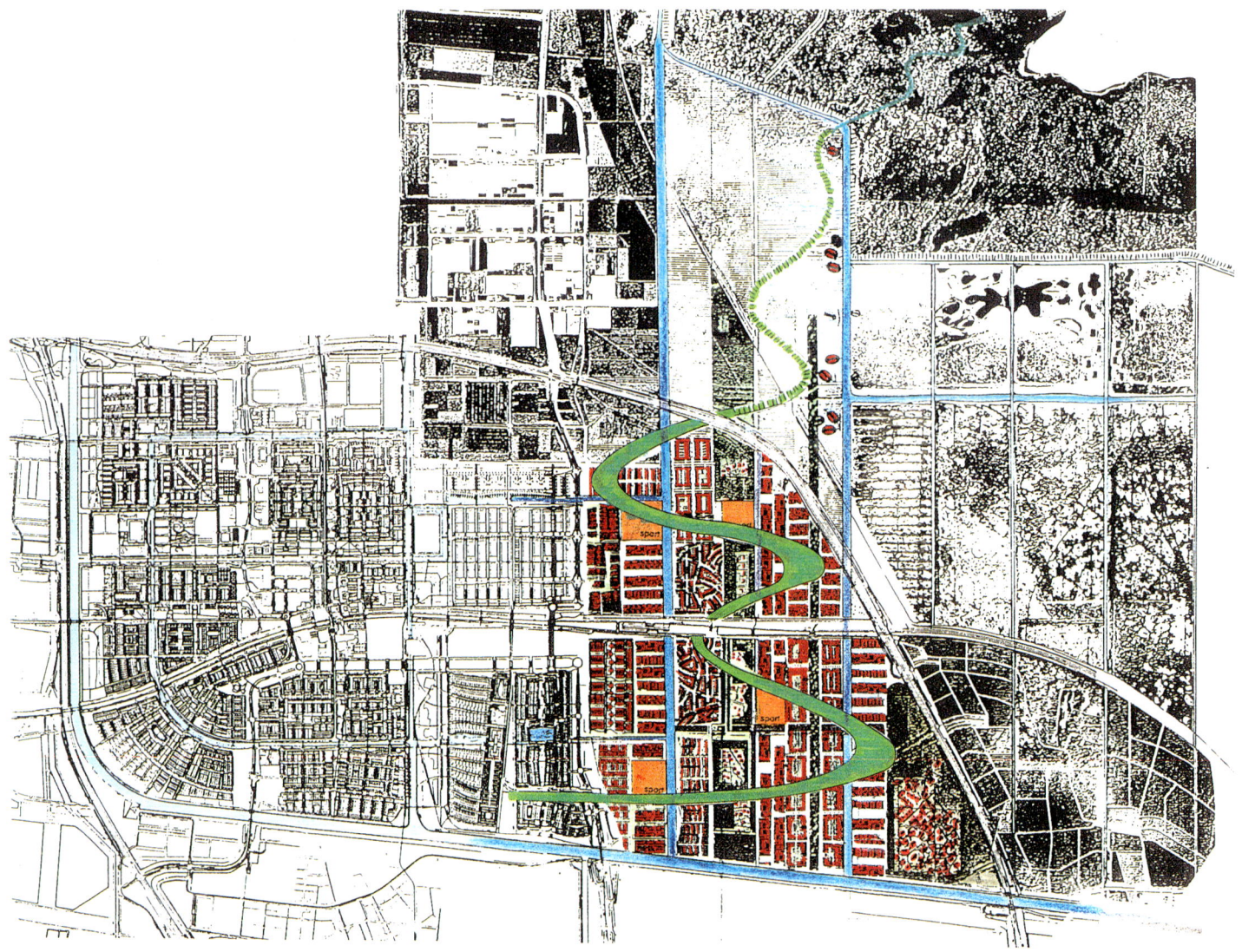

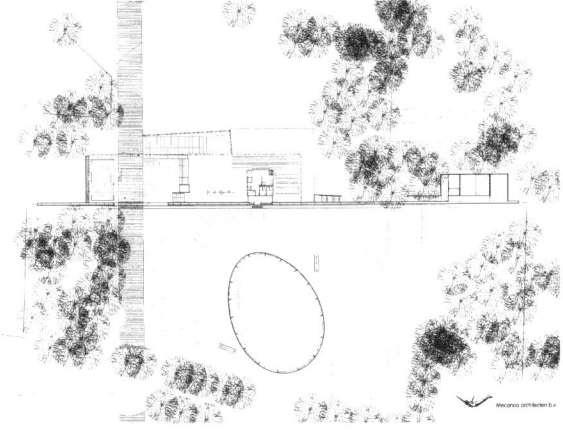

Is it a dinosaur egg or an erratic boulder millions of years old? Perhaps it is a futuristic, strange object placed here by men from Mars? A puzzling object of colossal proportions, partly sunk into the ground, stands in front of the entrance to the National Heritage Museum in Arnhem. You cannot enter it. To do that you must first go through a doorway in the dead straight, 143 metre long wall. But first of all you want to examine and feel that wall, experience the love of craftsmanship that radiates from it. The wall is an ode to the Dutch river landscape. The slowly flowing rivers leave a deposit of clay, and that clay has determined what the Netherlands looks like. There are bricks, bricks and more bricks. In many colours, structures and sizes. Not forgetting the enormous wealth of bonds and joint methods, such as moulded bricks in a quarter closer bond with a convex joint, blue glazed bricks in a fancy bond with a weathered joint, facing bricks in a stretcher bond with

Gesture in the landscape

a bastard tuck, sintered bricks in an irregular bond with burrs of mortar. You come across Dudok, Berlage and Mecanoo, as well as anonymous architects from over the centuries. The brick wall, the product of the Dutch river landscape, intersects the Waterberg and makes you feel the gently rolling wooded landscape on the northern side of Arnhem.

Meadow

The National Heritage Museum of Director Jan Vaessen

unfolds behind the wall. A large meadow is surrounded by beautiful trees, with a Delft windmill for grinding grain in the distance dating back to 1700, a small Gelderland farm from 1771 with an attractive front wall of bluish whitewash closer to hand, and the Zaan region from the seventeenth and eighteenth centuries just visible behind the lane of oak trees. This long Eikenlaan follows the contour of the meadow, intersects the pavilion, and determines the position of the gateway in the wall. The paving of the path goes literally through the building. The wall is finished on the inside of the pavilion with pure clay. It is a symbol of the durable techniques often applied in the traditional farms of Holland in the past.

The plan set in an aerial photograph

Pavilion

The 15 by 60 metre pavilion is an elongated, attractive, peaceful hall that follows the gradient of the site. The space is organised by two wooden boxes. One of them hovers above your head and houses the administrative part of the shop, the other stands on the ground and hides from view the service areas and kitchen that are required for the functioning of the restaurant and the auditorium. The hall is a large, multi-functional area that can cope with the large crowds (on peak days) while at the same time providing intimacy at quieter times. Lectures can be given there. The shop display and the counters are on mobile frames, so that everything can interlock like a compact box. You can descend on the large, round reading table with books and computers to investigate the museum collection in more depth.

Panorama

A large overhang prevents any sunlight from entering the pavilion. It is as if the building itself holds a hand above its eyes to be able to enjoy the view properly. The roof hangs like a projection from the wall. Almost invisibly, the – deep – laminated wooden struts arranged in an irregular pattern support the roof. As you walk to the restaurant and the auditorium, it is as if the glass pavilion is closed off and protected by the vertical strips. When seen from the opposite direction, however, the pavilion is completely transparent as it looks out on the wide panorama.

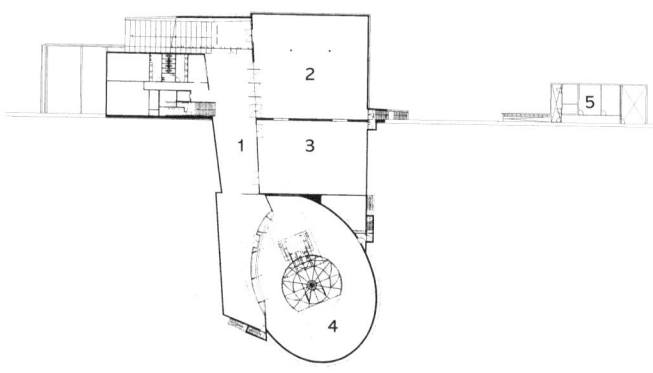

Basement

1. Lobby
2. Space for changing exhibitions
3. Space for costume exhibition
4. HollandRama
5. Technical space
6. Auditorium and cafe
7. Hydraulic stage floor
8. Museum shop

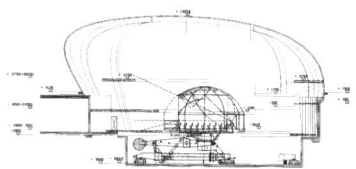 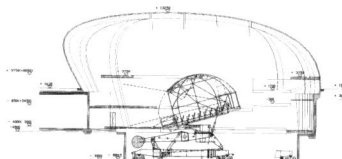 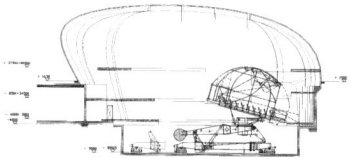 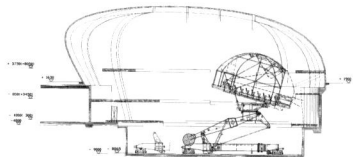

The moving platform

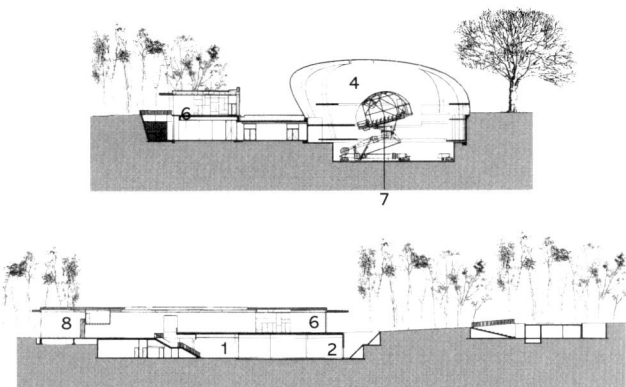

Cross-sections

Elegant
The floors of the pavilion are simple and elegant at the same time: coins and beads have been embedded in the concrete floor as small curiosities. An old cobbled floor is sunk into the concrete like a petrified carpet. Near the auditorium a crosscut oak floor creates a warm atmosphere. The different levels in the hall are designed like the staircase in a theatre. This transitional point marks the entrance to the underworld. Technical installations are integrated in the building. Everything is tucked away out of sight behind the wooden beams of the ceiling.

Underworld
The underworld is an artificial world. You can manipulate it, arrange and illuminate it to suit the time, subject and mood. The underworld cannot tolerate daylight. The smallest room houses the unique collection of local costume and jewellery, based on the collection of Queen Wilhelmina. Daylight would harm the delicate textiles. The main room is for temporary exhibitions, that are devoted to current social issues. The two rooms, fitted with modern equipment, offer an exhibition space of more than 800 m². The rooms are four metres high. All kinds of stands and frames can be erected there.

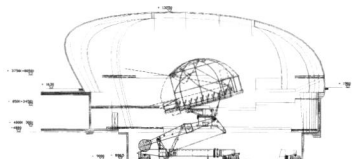 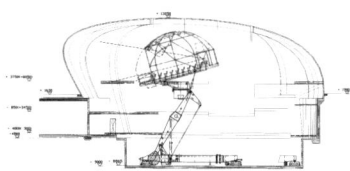 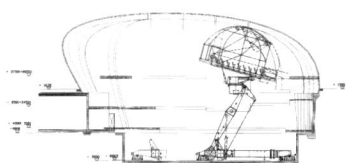 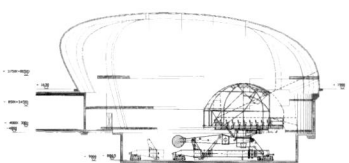

Solution

At the end of the underworld you see the boulder. The solution is close at hand. You enter it through the copper skin. A moving platform explores the possibilities of the interior of the enormous egg, 18 metres high, 20 metres wide and 40 metres long. You experience Dutch history together with 170 other visitors. The fears of the Second World War, the unique sound of skates on the frozen Dutch waters, the childlike cheery mood of the Queen's Birthday, the aroma of coffee, freshly ground by hand. Peace, nostalgia, cold, discomfort, beauty and sorrow. All emotions that colour Dutch history. The underworld makes it possible.

Upper world

You find the route back to the upper world by walking towards the light of day, where you see a sloping staircase. The most logical step is to take the wide stairs. They bring you to the outside world where the collection, with more than eighty buildings, is exhibited life size in the park. If you take the narrow stairs you find yourself back in the pavilion via a secret route. In both cases you are once again a part of the upper world, a composition of nature and architecture, of rigid lines and warm curves, where materials like copper, wood and clay are combined with stone, steel, concrete and glass.

The immediate environment of the new museum is designed as a landscape. Boulders beside the path serve as informal benches. The ticket office – the egg – mediates in scale between the monumental boulder and the erratic blocks. When evening falls it is all magically lit up. The wall, the egg and a few solitary trees. How beautiful it must be to return some time in the winter, when the snow has just fallen.

155. Entrance with the copper boulder
Fragment of wall
Boulder
156. Entrance hall with cobbled floor
157. Panorama looking towards the park with the meadow
The museum shop
158. HollandRama in the Boulder Underworld reception room with slope up to the outside world
159. The shell encasing the moving platform
160. As if the building itself holds a hand above its eyes to enjoy the view
View from the meadow
161. The irregular rhythm of the laminated wooden beams that support the roof
162. Entrance building with the 'Blue House' in the foreground
View from the meadow

First sketch collage

Maliebaan, around 1900

In 1897 the architect S.J. de Rooy designed a home for himself in the monumental Maliebaan in Utrecht. The detached residence has two storeys, a truncated hipped roof and a large garden. During the foundation of Utrecht University in 1636, the Maliebaan was designed as a pall-mall alley for students and professors so that they could indulge in this fourteenth-century sport to their heart's content.

The architect lived in the house until his death in 1916, and his widow Alida until 1931. They had no children, but a servant who lived on the premises. Afterwards the house accommodated the Catholic Youth Society, followed by S.F.H.J. Berkelbach

A house to work in

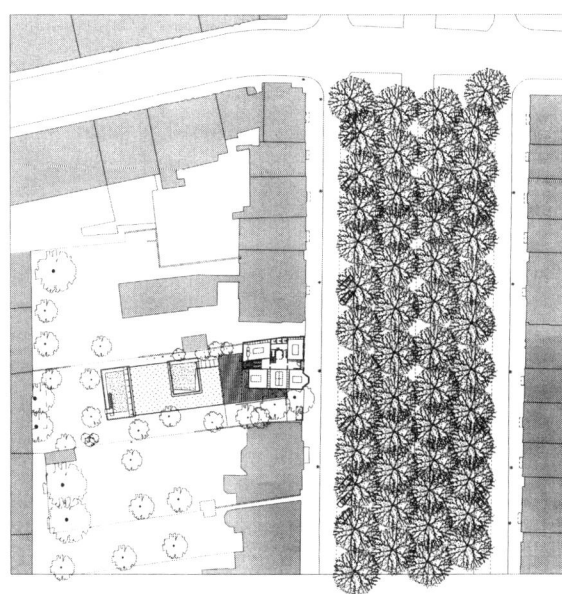

van der Sprenkel, a professor of theology, until the Kreisberg family came to live in it in 1952. J.H. Fentener van Vlissingen bought it in 1978 to use it as an office. That was when a stairway was built next to the villa to provide separate access to the attic, which had been converted into an apartment. In 1988 the management consultancy Andersson Elffers Felix took over the office.

In the course of the last fifty years all the spaciousness has gradually been removed from the villa. The ceilings have been lowered, and the premises have been expanded by 1.20 metres on the garden side. The stairway stands awkwardly beside it, with its crude wooden details that are so typical of the Seventies. The attic has been divided into small rooms with a bathroom and a kitchen. If you stand in the Maliebaan in the evening you can see which villas have been turned into offices from the rhythm of the fluorescent lights.

Villa

The first sketches of 4 October 1996 concentrate on giving prominence once again to the characteristics of a villa. Like its counterparts in Amsterdam and Delft, the house in the Maliebaan has survived all of the social changes since the end of the nineteenth century. The house must above all become a villa, not an office; a villa to work in and – who knows? – to live in later on: durable through the ages.

I want to fill the hall with daylight. The staircase must form the heart of the building in combination with this monumental hall. By using a different material and creating a different mood on each floor, you can reinforce the vertical structure of the villa. Of course, I want to harmonise natural light and artificial light. The lawn outside will have to be raised slightly to make room for an underground extension.

Underground

Our proposal to carry out an extension below the lawn and thus to maintain the garden proves to take a lot of time and force of conviction. Multiple use of the land is difficult in practice because of stubborn planning procedures. Is it a garden or a building? Eventually the plan receives the support and approval of the local authority in 1999 as an unusual proposal for intensive land use, which is appropriate to the future development of the city. In the meantime the restoration and renovation of the villa have already begun in 1998.

Durable

Renovation means removing a large volume of materials and bringing in a smaller volume of materials. Everything that has been brought into the villa in the last fifty years is taken out again. That is what the idea of durability means in practice in this building. A building has to stand up not only to many different users, but also to all architectural trends, and especially fashions in interior architecture and design.

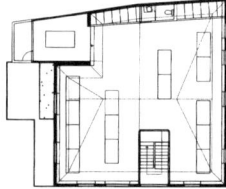
Second floor

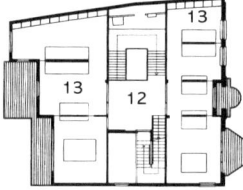
First floor

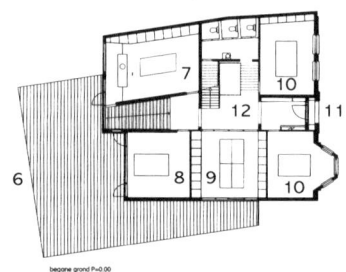
Ground floor

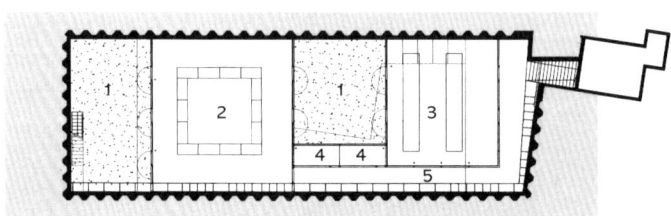
Underground extension with two patios

1. *Patio*
2. *Conference room*
3. *Working space*
4. *Telephones*
5. *Corridor*
6. *Terrace*
7. *Kitchen*
8. *Meeting room*
9. *Secretariat*
10. *Meeting room*
11. *Entrance*
12. *Hall*
13. *Working spaces*
14. *Balcony*

Three floors

A wonderful roomy hall, northern lights that enter through the new monastery windows, and the large wooden staircase form the heart of the building. The use of warm colours and materials with plenty of contrasts and the beautiful daylight that is filtered through the trees turn the villa into a house where it is pleasant to work. Light fittings are specially devised for the villa. The three floors acquire a surprising diversity, each with its own characteristic floor. The ground floor is like the floor of a ship's deck with oak planks and wenge borders, the first storey has an intense blue carpet, and the attic has stainless steel floor plates in which the special light from outside and the leaves are reflected.

The whole northern wall is covered with floor to ceiling cupboards, with a pattern of musical notes where the handles are. Behind them are the installations, a kitchen, a pantry, storage space, and above all lots of office cupboards and filing cabinets. The table tops are fitted for computers. Flexible work stations are the principle. The kitchen is the meeting place for everyone, with all mod cons, including a wall with magazines to leaf through.

Pond

Work on the underground pavilion commences in 1999: a spectacular job on a small city location. Big lorries come and go to remove 2,500 m³ of soil, while dam walls 11 metres long are sunk into the ground. After 500 m³ of underwater concrete have been tipped in, it looks as though there is a big pond in the garden. A waterproof connection with the cellar of the villa calls for a great deal of attention. When the water has finally been pumped out after thirteen weeks, the pavilion and the two patios are constructed in the following months and covered with a grass roof. Gravel is laid in the garden to the borders. Two green beeches and a copper beech are planted behind the pavilion to replace two adult chestnut trees in the course of time. Three oaks and a red chestnut tree have been planted naturally at random beside the drive. The trees, with a trunk 45 cm in diameter, have been selected from one of the best nurseries in Brabant. The garden has the elegance of an estate, in the middle of the inner city of Utrecht. Eighteen red acers in pots stand on the wooden terrace around the villa. By night the light on the trees turns the garden into a fairy-tale. The garden is separated from the Maliebaan by Linda Verkaaik's artistically designed gateway of steel bamboo.

Sketch steel bamboo gate by Linda Verkaaik

Root level

As you enter the villa, with the stately lime trees of the Maliebaan behind you, you take in the three core elements of Maliebaan 16 at a glance: the hall, the garden, and the pavilion. The oak ship's floor has been continued down over the easy stairs and leads to the underground extension. This pavilion consists of two large rooms and two patios. A fourteen-metre-long wooden wall with cupboards, hiding behind it the installations, cloakroom, office cupboards and drawers, pantry and audiovisual equipment, forms the boundary on the south side. The northern wall is made of smoothly cast concrete and catches the sunlight. All the other walls are made of glass. In the patio you experience – at root level – the huge dimensions of the centuries-old chestnut trees. Next to the open concrete staircase, a little distance from the concrete wall, the sculpture by Klaas Gubbels is set in the gravel. Now and then the sun creates a fantastic play of shadows, giving rise to a second work by the same artist.

167. *Villa seen from the garden, with the first patio in the foreground*
168. *View of the garden from the entrance Conference room*
169. *Garden by night Garden*
170. *Entrance underground pavilion*
171. *Central hall Attic with stainless steel floor sheets*
172. *The South wall: forty metres of cupboards*
173. *The North wall is made of perfectly cast concrete and catches the sun*
174. *In the patio you enjoy the immense scale of the time-hallowed chestnut trees at root level*

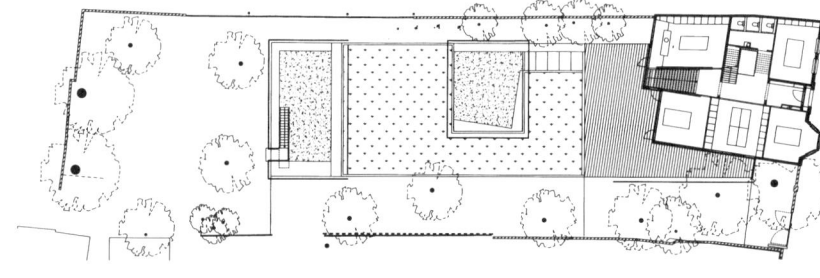

Ground plan of garden

Section

'Which opera is it?' is the question everyone asks when I tell them that we are working on the décor for an opera. Then I explain that it is a new opera. An opera is an opera, and they have all already been written, is the general opinion.

There are a number of stages in making a new opera. Flemish Dramatic Company-Transparant asks Johan Thielemans to write a libretto that has to be about the world of art. Johan Thielemans discusses the various possibilities with the Belgian composer Wim Henderickx. The theme of the artist in search of recognition appeals to him the most. Of course, they can identify with that theme. Johan Thielemans reads the story of an underrated painter in a French newspaper. The painter forges works by twentieth-century colleagues to take his revenge. His wife sells the works. Everything runs smoothly until he is caught. This scenario provides enough excitement and it raises the crucial question of talent, ability and originality. Thielemans

Triumph of Spirit over Matter

writes the libretto and Wim Henderickx writes the music for what is to be the opera *Triumph of Spirit over Matter*.

Hollandia

Transparant approaches Johan Simons and Paul Koek from The Hollandia Dramatic Company to direct the opera. This theatre company originally turned its back on the theatres and plays in temporarily or permanently abandoned buildings. In this way Hollandia allows the real world to play an important part. Weather and wind, smells and sounds, the light and sights from outside, are all deliberately used. Hollandia plays in the halls of the Westergasfabriek in Amsterdam, in a breaker's yard in Westzaan, beneath a traffic bridge in Antwerp, and, while work simply goes on, in the halls of KLM Cargo at Schiphol airport. The work becomes a part of the performance, reality becomes a part of the fiction. This is Hollandia's first opera. Johan Simons and Paul Koek give me a typewritten copy of the libretto and ask me to design the décor. They cannot let me hear the music yet. I read the libretto above the Atlantic on a flight to Detroit.

Chairs

The archetypal character of the personages leads me to make chairs the starting point of the décor. I choose four different chairs by Charles and Ray Eames, and one by Frank Gehry. Each of them has a pronounced character that can be personified. La Chaise with its flowing synthetic form – based on a seated woman with her legs extended sideways by Gaston Lachaise – is for the artist's wife Elsie. Frank Gehry's awkward Wiggle, a ribbon of folded packing carton, is for the artist Beck. The elegant office chair Aluminium is for gallery owner Gunther Dreck. The simple chromium steel mesh of Wire is for his secretary Frans Beacon. And the knotted tension of the natural wood of Plywood is for the journalist Theo. The chairs give the directors the opportunity to visualise the game of musical chairs around Elsie.

Décor

The two main rooms in the opera, the artist's studio and the gallery, consist of two gigantic chairs in contrasting materials, inspired by Gerrit Rietveld's zigzag chair. This accentuates, enlarges and gives prominence to the idea of getting chairs to personify the characters. The use of material gives form to the contrast between the two rooms: the artificial, electric blue wood of the gallery versus the natural, untreated bamboo of the studio. Using spotlights to bring out the irregularities of the bamboo produces an exciting play of light with wonderful shadow contours.

The characters

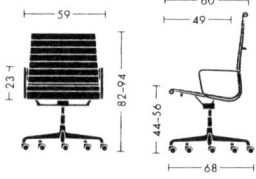

Gunther Dreck
The gallery owner

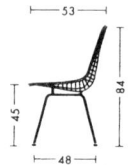 

Frank Beacon
The secretary of
the gallery owner

Theo
The journalist

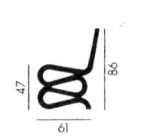

Beck
The artist

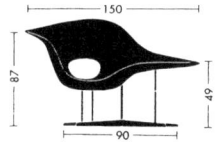

Elsie
The artist's wife

La Chaise of flowing cast plastic based on a seated woman with her legs extended sideways by Gaston Lachaise

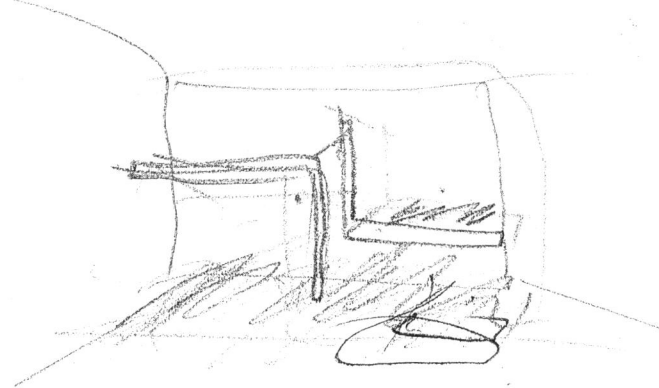

First sketch of décor with two rooms: studio and gallery

Rehearsals

The world première is scheduled for Brussels on 10 March 2000. The weeks preceding it go by quickly. We make a scale model of the décor in December, make a definitive choice of the chairs in January, and produce the décor in February. The orchestra starts rehearsing in Belgium in February and the English and Dutch opera singers do the same in the Netherlands. Ten days before the première the décor is set up in a small theatre out of town to enable the singers to rehearse with the décor and piano. I hold my breath. Three days before the première it is all transported to Brussels and I can breathe again. The décor looks impressive in the bare stage area. We have removed all the curtains to get the feeling of being on location and to ensure good acoustics for the singers. The lighting has to be much more dramatic, extreme, varied. The orchestra appears with fragments of music, the singers are still in their working clothes. They rehearse with a lot of interruptions.

179. The bamboo chair is the studio space
180. The première
182. Play of light of the irregular bamboo

Applause

We have to hurry to make it to the première – what the Belgians call the 'world creation' – because there is an enormous traffic jam between Rotterdam and Brussels. We slip into the packed auditorium and head for our reserved seats. The conductor raps his baton, the light gradually becomes more intense, and we hear the music of the Prometheus Ensemble. The singers sing and act brilliantly. The décor works as it is designed to work: a fantastic space enabling the play of light. We all appear on stage at the end of the performance. The combination of all the different disciplines determines the success of an opera. It is unusual to see how that is all put together in such a brief period of time. Applause!

Afterwards we splash out on a big dinner in the royal room of the Munt opera house. One of the speakers is so impressed by the décor that he wonders whether the opera should have been called Triumph of Matter over Spirit.

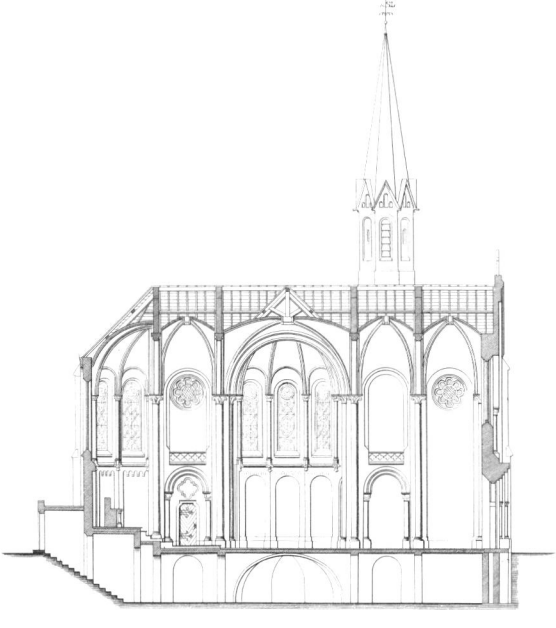

First chapel, 1880

November 1998. I am about to leave for Venice. The telephone rings. It is father Joost de Lange asking if I would like to design a chapel for a cemetery. It has to be ready for use in the year 2000. He does not want to tell me the location yet. We make an appointment for after my return. I cannot shake off the request in Venice: a chapel for the year 2000! I am there with art historian Jan van Adrichem. He takes me to the many chapels and churches of Venice for three days. He tells me about Byzantine Gothic, Early and High Renaissance, Baroque and Rococo, the paintings of Titian with their dramatic light effects, the fourteen stations, and the Chapel of Mary. I study the ground plans. I sit and dream in every chapel. What atmosphere do I want to create? What is the specific element of a funeral for me?

St Mary of the Angels

Venetian dream

Three days later, Jan van Adrichem laughs as he asks me what my chapel will look like. I reply cautiously but very firmly. 'I have a dream that is not complete yet, because the location is missing, but I know the ingredients. It must be a jewel casket, with a big expressive roof, a golden canopy and a beam of light. I am thinking of a blue, continuous, narrative wall. And the chapel will be a part of a route, which in turn is a part of a ceremony: a ceremony of standing still, reflecting, and then going on again, as a symbol of the life that goes on. I don't want a dead end chapel. And it must be intimate, whether it is for ten or a hundred people.'

Immediately upon my return I have my first meeting with the pastor and his board at the Rotterdam episcopacy. I blurt out my Venetian dream. They show me the location and invite me to imagine the chapel of my dreams.

Cemetery with first chapel

Transience

I am walking in the Roman Catholic cemetery of St Lawrence in Rotterdam. I go through the porch in a wall and enter an atmosphere of transience, of old trees and graves. In the middle a chapel is on the point of collapse, beside a dilapidated arcade. Faded photographs of a very different chapel, a kind of small church, hang in the porch. I am curious about the history.

The cemetery replaced the St Lawrence cemetery around St Lawrence church in the centre of Rotterdam. That cemetery had to make way for the vegetable market in 1680. Catholics were buried in the church itself until 1830, when it was no longer allowed for reasons of hygiene. The Catholics urgently needed a new cemetery. The donation of the former estate of Groenendaal facilitated the construction of a Roman Catholic cemetery. It was opened on 13 March 1865.

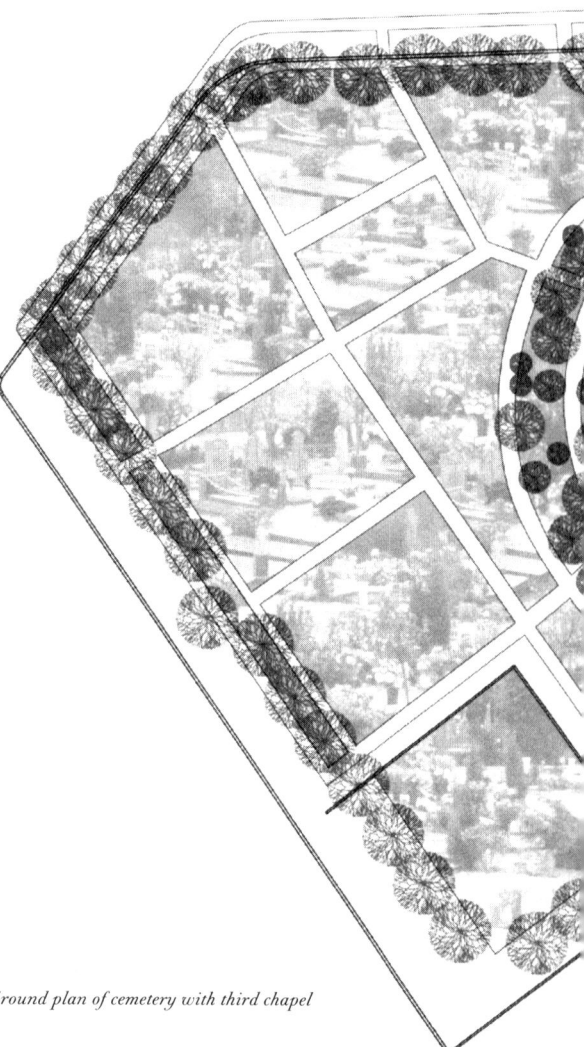

Ground plan of cemetery with third chapel

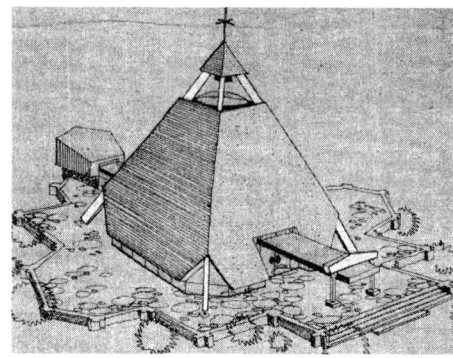

Second chapel, 1963

Campo Santo

The architect H.J. van den Brink designed the cemetery as an Italian field of the dead, a campo santo. He was a disciple of the architect P.J.H. Cuypers and had a reputation as an architect of churches in Neo-Classical style. This was also the style in which he designed the porches and a chapel situated in the centre, which were connected with one another by a straight lane. The chapel was surrounded by a circular path with main paths radiating from it. A Neo-Romanesque arcade on top of double burial chambers was built around the perimeter of the cemetery.

Unstable ground

The roof of the original arcade was removed thirty years ago because of its poor condition. The Neo-Classical chapel, which was opened in 1869, had subsided because of the bad quality of the subsoil. Given the risk of its collapsing, it was decided to demolish it. A new chapel was constructed on the vaults of the old one in 1963: a building shaped like a large Indian tent, covered with copper, with a clock at the top. It is incredible, but this chapel was affected by foundation problems as well. Once again there was a risk of collapse and the chapel had to be demolished. So we are designing the third chapel for the Roman Catholic cemetery of St Lawrence in Rotterdam; this time with a new foundation.

187. Scale model
188. Remains of the foundations
of the first chapel by
H.J. van den Brink
190. Scale model

Golden ceiling

The routing of the chapel is based on trust in the continuation of life. You carry the deceased into the chapel, have a moment of reflection in a quiet, meditative building, and then leave the chapel in a single, continuous movement. The space has an organic form: a continuous, curving wall, raised seventy centimetres above the ground. The wall has an intense colour, with texts from the Requiem in many languages; the cemetery is a place for the multicultural population of Rotterdam. The roof floats like a folded sheet of paper above the space. The golden ceiling is artificially lit from below. An opening in the ceiling allows daylight to enter the chapel in a bundle of light that is further accentuated at the moment when incense is used. The chapel stands on a plateau of gravel within the contours of the previous Neo-Classical chapel. Two heated, wooden decks indicate the place of the priest and the congregation. The clock from the 1963 chapel hangs in the tower. The chapel of St Mary of the Angels is like a precious jewel and a beautiful example of palimpsest: a roll of parchment that has been reused after the previous text has been erased or covered up.

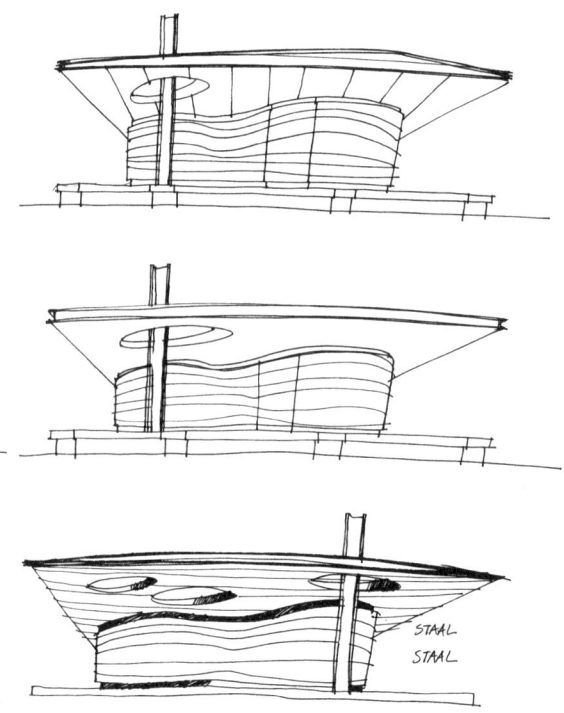

Design sketches for chapel

Rotterdam sprang up at the confluence of the Maas and the Rotte. The port, the economic development and the high-rise buildings of Rotterdam are closely connected with the River Maas. The Rotte, the small river from which Rotterdam takes its name, is popular for recreational purposes because of its green and watery surroundings of pools and lakes. Wedged between the twisting, romantic Rotte and the linear noise barrier of the motorway lies Nieuw Terbregge. This inner city Vinex location is situated on a typically Dutch site where the water level is higher than the land. The development of the district is part of the Thermie-project, a European model project in which eight European cities develop innovative, sustainable housing projects.

Vinex
Since the publication of the Fourth Memorandum Extra on

Between the Rotte and the motorway

Town and Country Planning in 1990, a change has taken place in Dutch housing. From the production of rented property – often council housing commissioned by the housing associations – to the production of owner occupied property commissioned by project developers. The ideal of the Vinex district is: everyone has their own house and their own garden. However, you can follow the discussions of the Vinex locations every day in the Netherlands on the radio and in the press. Architects are generally not impressed, politicians are divided, while the occupants – usually the owners – are satisfied. To a large extent it is an unclear discussion. What is it about? The programme? The image? Style, modern or classicist? Monotonous rows of houses? The absence of individual clients? All those parked cars? Is space a scarce commodity in the Netherlands or not? I find these questions secondary or uninteresting, at any rate they do not go to the heart of the matter. In my view, what is missing in the Vinex districts is a vision that is a response to the present day, in which sustainability, mobility, and the home-work-recreation house are important perspectives. I want to come up with an answer by showing, by building what I mean.

Mobility

Environmental planners have been stuck with the car for decades: the car is a mistake and the use of the car must be reduced. This means that when new residential neighbourhoods are being created, the politicians – and the local city planners – must keep parking down. This turns out to be like putting your head in the sand. The next step is that the way the districts look is dominated by an overabundance of parked cars, no matter how all those architects have done their best with what is often neat and tidy – too rigid – architecture.

Mobility is an essential part of modern society, but environmental pollution is a serious problem. Attempts to reduce it since the mid-Seventies through environmental planning have been in vain. Significant results in the reduction of air pollution can be achieved by technical innovations to the car itself. I want to point out the need for an aesthetic of mobility. At the same time I want to take up the challenge of developing a new typology that integrates the intrinsic role of mobility on the scale of a neighbourhood.

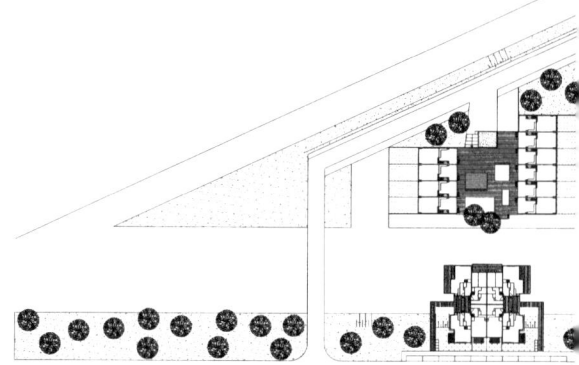

Ground plan housing estate

Tension

At the start of the design process for Nieuw Terbregge, I think about our previous work, the Ringvaartplasbuurt Oost in Prinsenland, not very far away. We are working with the same client, Peter van der Gugten, who has now become a project developer together with Piet Proper. The times have changed, and so has the market. The residents of the Ringvaartplasbuurt like living there; bus loads of architectural tourists go to have a look there, the children play excitedly and in safety. It is going well. The density, the number of houses per hectare, is higher in Nieuw Terbregge than in the Ringvaartplasbuurt. The prices of the owner occupied properties are high, the parcels of land are small. It is only when there is a lot of tension that you go in search of far-reaching solutions. Perhaps that is the trouble with the Vinex districts: there is no tension, it all just fits on the tiny plots of land overloaded with programme.

The programme for the Nieuw Terbregge location by the Rotterdam Local Authority is 70% ground level houses and 30% apartments. The client would prefer 100% ground level houses. I find the solution in this force field: I will stack not houses, but ground levels!

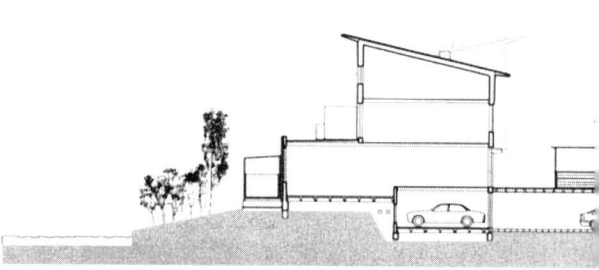

Cross-sections

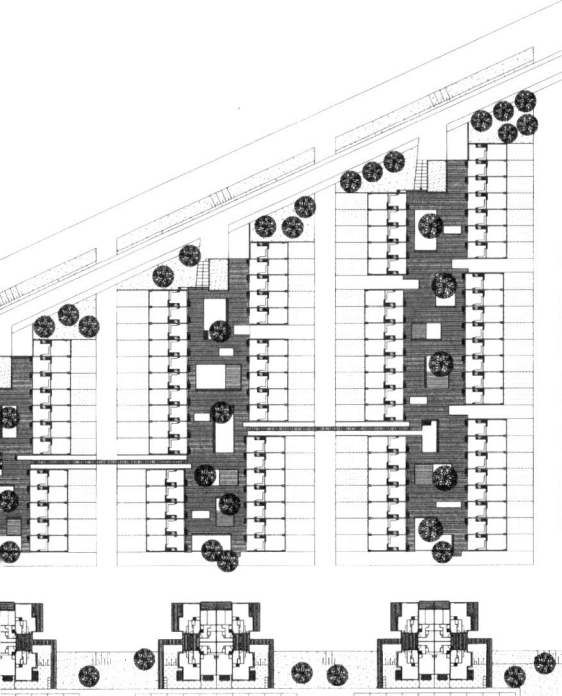

Adventure

It becomes four islands in the water, with four different sizes, from large to small. Four double-deckers with a double ground level: a wooden level for children on top of a stone one for cars. The two worlds are connected with one another by trees that grow through holes in the wooden level and staircases placed here and there. The gaps between the wooden planks of the platform built in the traditional scaffolding manner let filtered light through to the stone level.

The islands are connected with one another by a jungle bridge. The bridge hangs lazily from platform to platform. They are a protest against the tidiness of the Vinex neighbourhoods, which lack any adventure. Here is a neighbourhood where you can run and roll between the double-deckers, play hide and seek, jog along horizontal and vertical routes, or hold a barbecue in the street as if you are on holiday at home. But you can work there as well. You never go indoors through the front door, but always through the kitchen. The front door is for 'special' visitors.

Composition

While Prinsenland has dancing blocks, Nieuw Terbregge is given dancing roofs. The rhythm of the slightly irregular blocks in combination with the dancing roofs ensures a coherent composition for each island. The staccato of the alternation – per half house – between dark brown, unpolished wood and uncompromising white plaster brings about a visual interruption and refinement of the dimensions of the typical Dutch house in a row. It is a surprise to find hatches in the larchwood panelling of the outside wall. If you open them, air and light enter. The floor of the living kitchen flows into the platform without a break. The living room makes the jump towards the garden and the water, making it a wonderful high room. The swing-up door of the garage is designed to be one with the wooden front door. Perhaps it will become a workshop or a studio in the future.

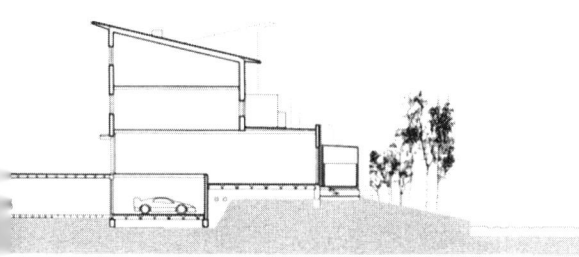

Chaos

The double-decker is highly organised, everything is arranged centrally as in a big block of flats: a mini boiler room, a container room for waste, the lighting of the trees on the platform, the position of the cables and piping. An Owners Association ensures that everything runs smoothly. The back wall is orange-brown masonry with white varnished wooden frames and a small unaligned window as a detail. More scope for chaos has been deliberately created on the ditch side: different levels, gardens, landing stages in the water. The future layer of green will gradually cover it in the future.

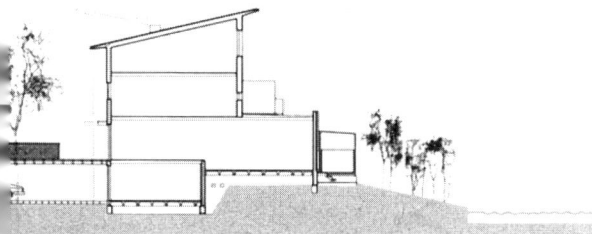

195. *Informal - second - entrance to the apartments from the platform*
196. *Stone level for cars*
198-199. *Jungle bridges connect the platforms with one another*
200. *Wooden platform for children*
202. *The platform as a place to enjoy with pergolas*

Eight under one roof

On the other side of the water are the eight under one roof waterfront houses, a concept that we had developed a few years earlier – with the same client – in the Rijkerswoerd district of Arnhem. In the position of both urban planner and architect, we are able to devise an alternative to the standard row of houses in the inexpensive category with which the Netherlands has been filled for decades. These waterfront houses consist of groups of eight units which combine to look like a large villa. They are not apartments but ground level houses, each with its own garden or platform above the water. The typology is an ingenious combination. The four intermediate houses are cheaper, the corner ones are more expensive. In Arnhem we placed these villas, surrounded by a ring of hedgerows, in an orchard. Here in Rotterdam they are half in the water.

Richness

The success of the double-deckers and the waterfront houses are proof to me of the need for new, contemporary housing typologies. It only makes sense to start out on this voyage of discovery if you are connected with a project as both architect and urban planner and cooperate with the client who is behind it.

You wonder how we have forgotten the richness of European urban planning typologies for housing. The house with a garden and one or two parking lots seems to be the highest good in the Netherlands. We will have to design houses that, like the Dutch residences of the seventeenth century, can cope with the major changes in society over the centuries. And above all: they will have to integrate the acquisition of mobility – the car – in our new urban planning typologies.

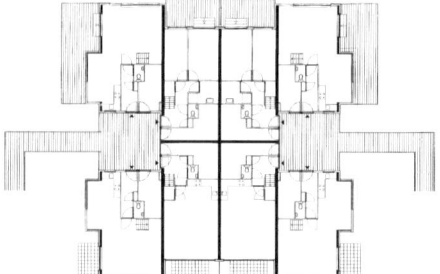

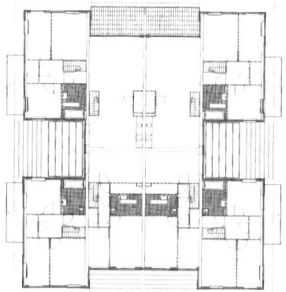

Floor plans 'eight under one roof'

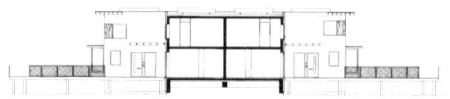

Section 'eight under one roof'

For years the Parkhotel has been established in one of the many monumental nineteenth-century villas beside the Westersingel in Rotterdam. The hotel started out as a family hotel, but in the course of time it has expanded in different directions through the purchase of adjacent villas and the construction of a wing in the garden. In 1984 the Hobokentoren by the architect Drexhage is added to the series of villas. In 1990 we draw up a master plan for a replacement and expansion of the existing premises in stages,

Rhapsody in Blue

in which we remove the villa next to the Hobokentoren and replace it by an executive tower. The sculptural zinc building is completed in 1992. The tower has only five rooms on each floor, leans against the Hobokentoren, and seems to be challenging it to see which is the biggest, the slimmest and the fairest. In combination they embody the progress and dynamism of Rotterdam.

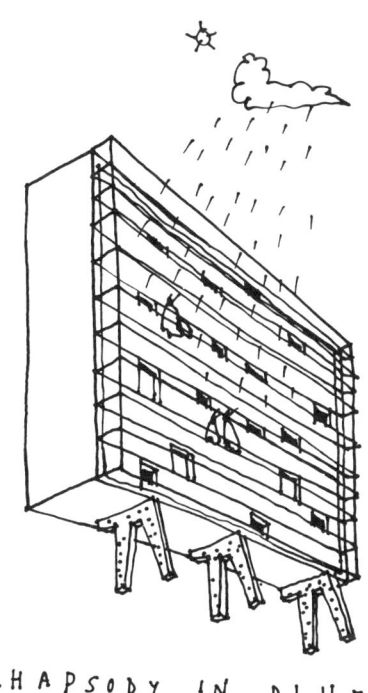

Sketch of North wall

New insight

In 1998 we decided with our client Peer Hosman from the Bilderberggroep and Henk Priem, the manager of the Parkhotel, that the master plan needs altering. In 1990 we had planned to eventually demolish the oldest part of the hotel and the garden wing and to replace them by new buildings. By 1998 we do no longer think this is such a good idea. It would be a pity to knock down this part, the symbol of the old family hotel with its strong ties with the city of Rotterdam. Enough has been destroyed in Rotterdam already. In fact, we derive more and more pleasure from the fact that the hotel is a mishmash of buildings – a city in the city. We continue this concept in the new master plan, the architecture, the interior and the pricing of the rooms. We leave the old buildings intact and plan an extension on the small car park that will fit into the jigsaw puzzle of the hotel complex.

North wall: the electric blue corridor appears behind a sheet of glass

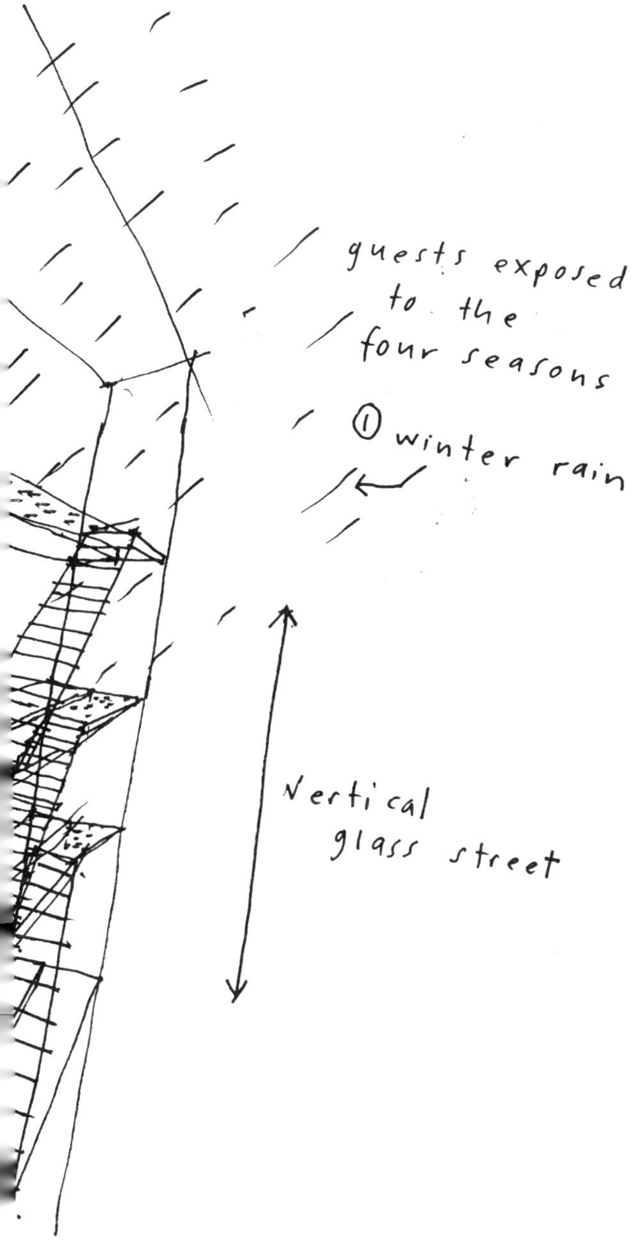

guests exposed to the four seasons

① *winter rain*

Vertical glass street

Enclave

The Parkhotel forms a small enclave in the city, a city that is never complete. The different periods are visible in this enclave. Each part has its own mood, styling and design. Inside too you feel that you are walking through different buildings. This is the value of the addition in the year 2001, and it is what gives this addition an atmosphere and identity of its own as well. Eventually the Parkhotel, that is primarily orientated towards the Westersingel, will come to be orientated towards the Rochussenstraat with its most public part: a new restaurant overlooking the city and directly opposite the flats and offices that we have designed on the corner of the Rochussenstraat. At right angles to the restaurant is a slender, rectangular wedge containing the bedrooms. This block is nine storeys high with six rooms per storey. The rooms face west with a fantastic view of the Museumpark. The wall on the side of the park is like a vast upright 30 x 30 metre painting. The windows are staggered like musical notes. It becomes an impressive stone wall of warm, orange-red brick. The adjacent Villa Sonneveld (1933) with the big garden designed by Brinkman and Van der Vlugt forms a splendid contrast with it.

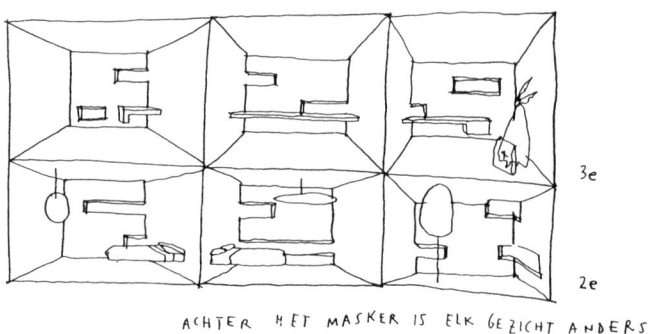

Sketch of the bedroom block

Intimacy

The location is so small that the bedroom block consists of only a single row of six rooms with one corridor. It is as if the hotel has been sliced in two and exposes its interior to the city. The electric blue corridor can be seen behind a sheet of glass. The doors of the rooms are clearly visible. The wall of glass hangs in front of them like a veil. Horizontal, aluminium lines form a rhythm in the glass construction. Rhapsody in Blue.

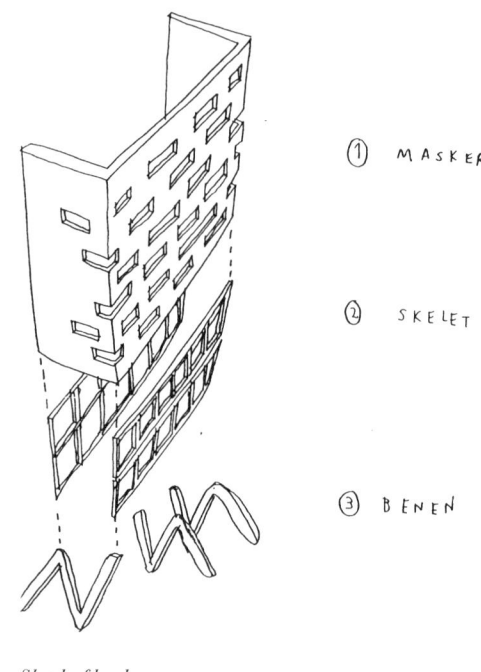

Sketch of hotel structure

207. *Bird's-eye view of location: Parkhotel with surrounding white villas, Rochussenstraat building and Museumpark*
208. *View from Eendrachtsplein*
209. *Parkhotel becomes a park of little hotels*
210. *South wall from Museumpark South wall from Rochussenstraat*

In 1999 we are inundated with requests to design exhibitions, including an invitation for the 4th Bienal Internacional de Arquitetura in São Paulo, Brazil. A question I have been thinking about for some time is: how can you design an architectural exhibition that is beautiful and compelling at the same time? I do not want to hang a book on the wall. It must be an exhibition where you can spend five minutes, five quarters of an hour or five hours looking, walking and sitting down, depending on your interest. The visitor must experience the Mecanoo feeling and the multi-layered structure of the work. If the exhibition is international, you will have to make secondary use of language. You have to be able to grasp the spatial dimension of our projects from almost

Mecanoo Blue

1
Bienal Internacional de Arquitetura,
São Paulo

10,000 kilometres away. The scale model is the best way to show and explain architecture.

Oscar Niemeyer
The international architectural biennial in São Paulo is intended to offer a panorama of what is going on nationally and internationally, not just for professionals but also for the general public. The exhibition is held in the fantastic Palace of Industry, a large exhibition pavilion from 1954 designed by Oscar Niemeyer. It is an impressive building with 35,000 m² of exhibition space in the middle of Roberto Burle Marx's Parque do Ibirapuera. No less than 25 international and 35 Brazilian exhibitions will be on show there at the same time. We are offered 250 m² of space on the second floor.

Scale models

We add four new scale models to our collection specially for this exhibition: the library of Delft Technical University; the Ringvaartplasbuurt Oost residential neighbourhood in Rotterdam; the house cum studio in Rotterdam; and the Almelo Public Library.

The model of the library of Delft Technical University is the masterpiece of our exhibition. This 'life-sized' scale model is made in the model workshop of the Department of Architecture of the Technical University on a scale of 1:50. We show the inside and the outside simultaneously. The grass roof with the glass porch, the spatial construction of the hall, and the interior of the cone can all clearly be seen. The bookcases and tables are made meticulously to scale. The lighting comes from the columns, just as it does in the actual library.

The 550 houses in Ringvaartplasbuurt Oost dance on a scale of 1:200. The model shows the beauty of a composition of repetition. The high-rise tower block rises like a ship amid the sea of houses. The four common landscape gardens and the hedges of the individual houses give an impression of the public space.

The house cum studio is pulled off by model builder Henk Bouwer. The scale of 1:20 forces him to recreate almost every detail of the house, indoors and outdoors. The model shows the use of different materials, such as the concrete and natural stone floors and the wooden staircase. The wall of cupboards, the concrete table, the floating kitchen cupboard and even the carpets have been made with a love of detail. He gets the children to make their own drawings to scale, and they hang like a big painting on the kitchen wall.

The 1:50 scale model of Almelo Public Library is a more conceptual model, with the curved outside wall and the split level construction of the different floors as the main ingredients of the plan.

These four models form the impressive core of the exhibition.

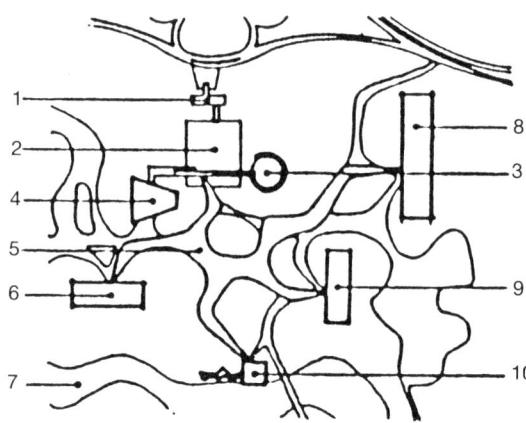

Ground plan the Awning

Giraffa

Sixteen crates are shipped to São Paulo. Fourteen models on blue pedestals are placed on a large blue carpet. We make a red reading table, 8 metres long and 2 metres wide, and arrange thirty Giraffa chairs by Lina Bo Bardi around it. There are eleven hand-made, bound books with sketches and information about the projects on the table. We place a wall of fresh Brazilian bamboo, 18 metres long and 5 metres tall, in front of the enormous glass wall. The bamboo screen filters the light in a subtle and irregular fashion and is used to exhibit 37 very sharp, glossy photographs. Six monitors play compilations of television programmes about Mecanoo projects. They are part of a 24-metre blue wall illustrating twenty years of Mecanoo history with drawings, sketches, photographs, materials, statements and texts that I have written by hand.

Awning

Our exhibition – along with sixty others – is put up in a week. During that week I get to know Oscar Niemeyer's building intimately. I have never seen such a severe building that at the same time accommodates such a dynamic interior. The undulating shapes of the wonderful empty hall, the grid of the columns that stand ten metres apart, the spiral slopes on which forklift trucks juggle their enormous loads to the different levels.

The atmosphere is chaotic and overwhelming at the same time. We build the whole Dutch submission together with Hannie van Eyck, Max Risselada, Herman Hertzberger and a whole team of architects and assistants. We work at a feverish pace and our muscles start to ache from walking up and down the slopes. We eat together in the kilo restaurant – you pay for your food by its weight – beneath Oscar Niemeyer's awning: a covered pedestrian route with an organic ground plan, whose enormous wavy roof serves as an umbrella and parasol and which links the pavilions and museums in the park with one another. Every day I admire the power of the exhibition pavilion and of the awning. An unforgettable experience.

Parque do Ibirapuera

Arquitetura Award

The opening ceremony is held on 20 November 1999. The curators Lúcio Gomes Machado and Luiz Fisberg walk down from the second floor over the slope with a large retinue of South American architects and politicians. It is a wonderfully dramatic sight. Mecanoo Blue is transformed into a crowded gallery. People sit at the table all the time. They read the books, watch the videos, stand beside the models for hours and – to my amazement – they even read the whole blue wall. The Brazilian bamboo and Lina Bo Bardi's chairs feel at home in our exhibition space. The Bienal is a big success and attracts more than 150,000 visitors. Our exhibition draws a lot of attention and the impressive models are picked up by several television stations. As the reward for our efforts, Mecanoo Blue receives the *4th Bienal Internacional de Arquitetura* Award.

Afterwards our exhibition travels to the Museo Nacional de Bellas Artes in Buenos Aires, Argentina.

215. The bamboo wall filters the light
Empty area in the Palace of Industry during the 4th Bienal Internacional
216. The model of the Delft Technical University Library
Models on a blue carpet
217. Fragment of the 24-metre wall with 20 years of Mecanoo history
Reading table with 'Giraffa' chairs by Lina Bo Bardi
218. Model Ringvaartplasbuurt Oost, Prinsenland, Rotterdam
Detail of bamboo wall

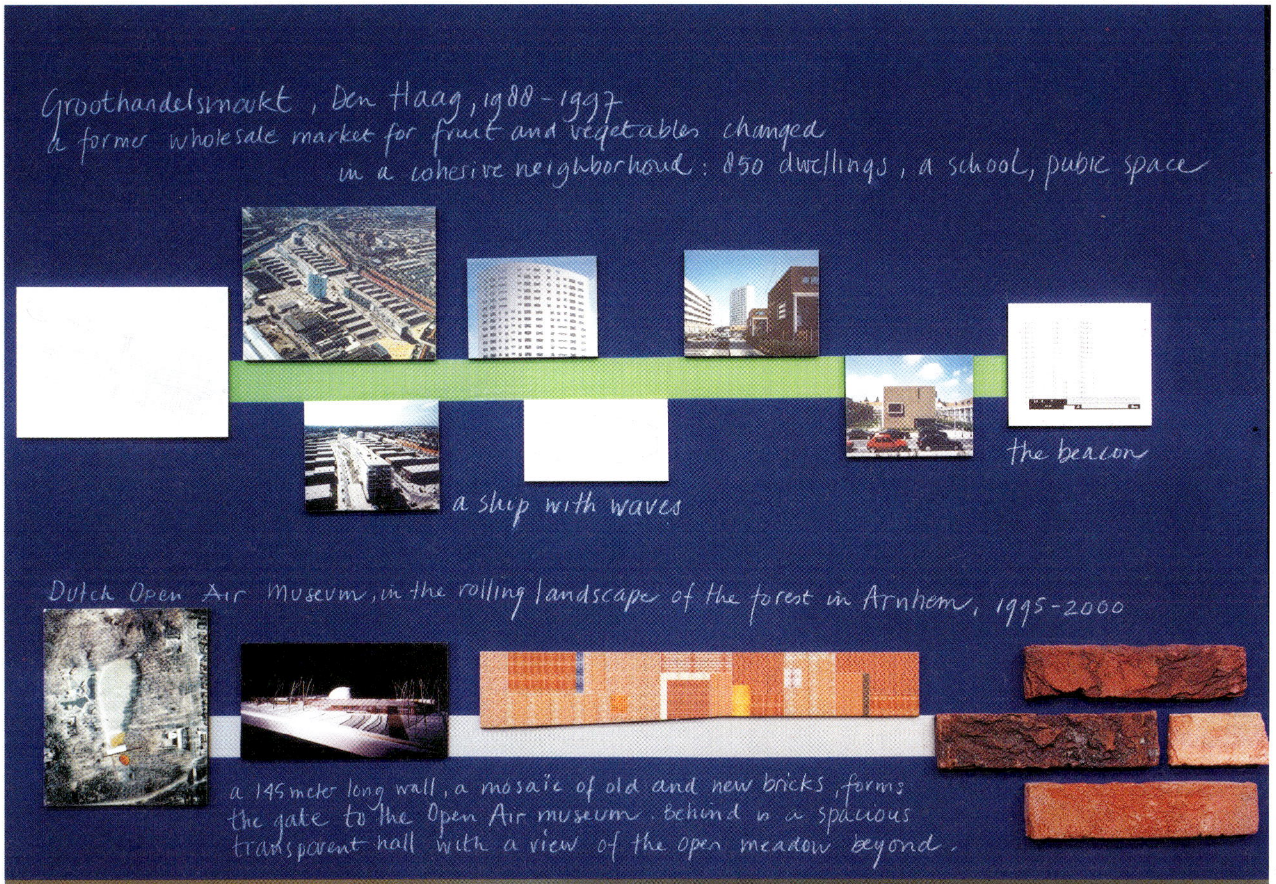
Groothandelsmarkt, Den Haag, 1988-1997
a former wholesale market for fruit and vegetables changed
in a cohesive neighborhoud: 850 dwellings, a school, public space
a ship with waves
the beacon
Dutch Open Air museum, in the rolling landscape of the forest in Arnhem, 1995-2000
a 145 meter long wall, a mosaic of old and new bricks, forms
the gate to the Open Air museum. Behind is a spacious
transparent hall with a view of the open meadow beyond.

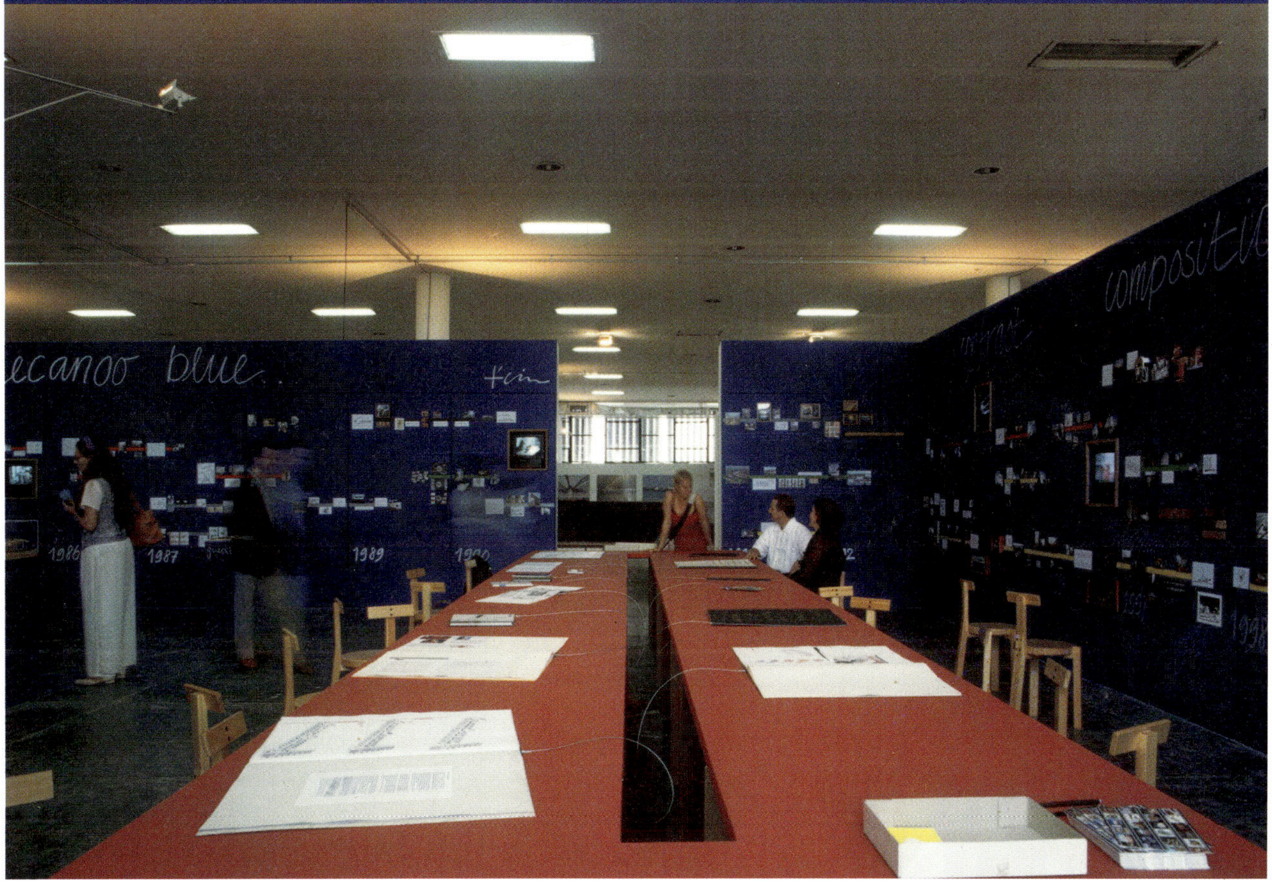
ecanoo blue
1986
1987
1989

The Netherlands has a rich tradition when it comes to water management and hydraulic engineering. For centuries engineers have been working on dykes, drainage, cleverly devised locks and bridges. While the Ministry of Transport, Public Works and Water Management used to be concerned with large-scale hydraulic works, nowadays its main focus is infrastructure and mobility, and whereas economic and technical possibilities used to determine how engineers thought, economics and the market seem to be the determinant factors today.

Major investments in infrastructure will lead to new and modified routes of motorways and railway lines in the landscape. The future of the most malleable country in the world offers a new opportunity for a vision of how the space around the main Dutch routes for through traffic is organised. I argue for an aesthetics of mobility in order to guarantee an attractive public space for the Netherlands.

A room with a view

A room with a view

Collective responsibility
The Netherlands is a country with a very strong tradition in the field of collective responsibility for the water. Unambiguous agreements regulate the management of land and water – literally, because otherwise we would all drown. The tradition of collective responsibility for water management could easily be extended to a collective responsibility for the sustainability of how the country is ordered. After all, that too is a question of the survival of us all.

The most malleable country in the world
The Dutch landscape is characterised by wonderful, changing typologies. The cities are constantly developing, and the landscape is not static either, it is malleable and changeable. The contrasts between order and chaos, polders and lakes, canals and wetlands, dykes and river forelands, wet and dry, are the elements that you can use in the Netherlands to give shape to the landscape.

The Netherlands is the most malleable country in the world, but this strength is also its weakness. There are no limits. It seems as if with the help of engineers you can build anywhere. The land has become so malleable that you can destroy it too.

Towards a new art of engineering

The Department of Public Works will have to shift its attention from individual works of art to complete trajectories in the future. This calls for a new style of working. The most interesting and valuable developments in architecture are given a chance if we manage to break out of the current fragmented practice of design and building in order to create the freedom to experiment and to work together. Surprising combinations of disciplines lead to inventiveness and new insights. On the large scale of the infrastructure, road and hydraulic engineers, landscape architects and architects can work together to develop an innovative vision for the long term. This means experimenting with combined programmes, constructions, water and materials, but emphatically without the loss of the architect's own role and responsibility.

Hello, here I am

No city can get by without motorways. At the same time it hates them. They are impregnable barriers and noisy ribbons which have to be increasingly wrapped up in noise barriers. The opposite can be seen outside the city. Buildings seem to have a preference for the motorway, they edge towards it. Through their format and design they call out: 'Hello, here I am.' They and the industrial hangars constitute the hated ribbon development alongside the motorways.

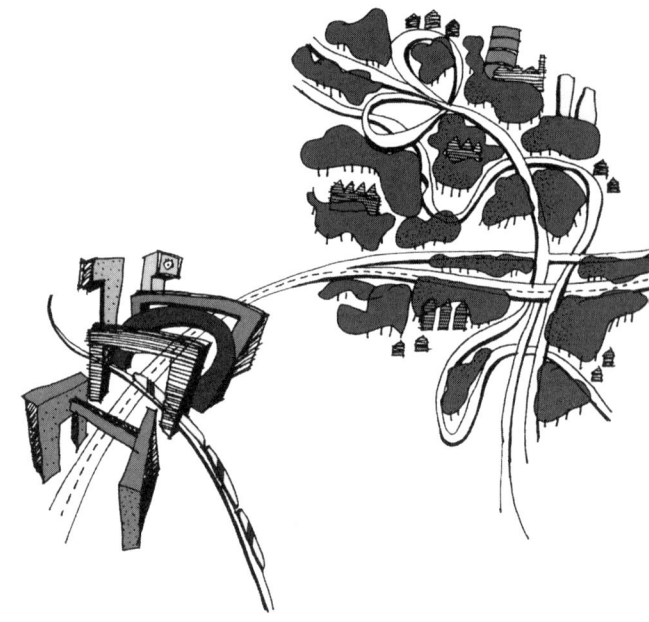

Composition of six typologies

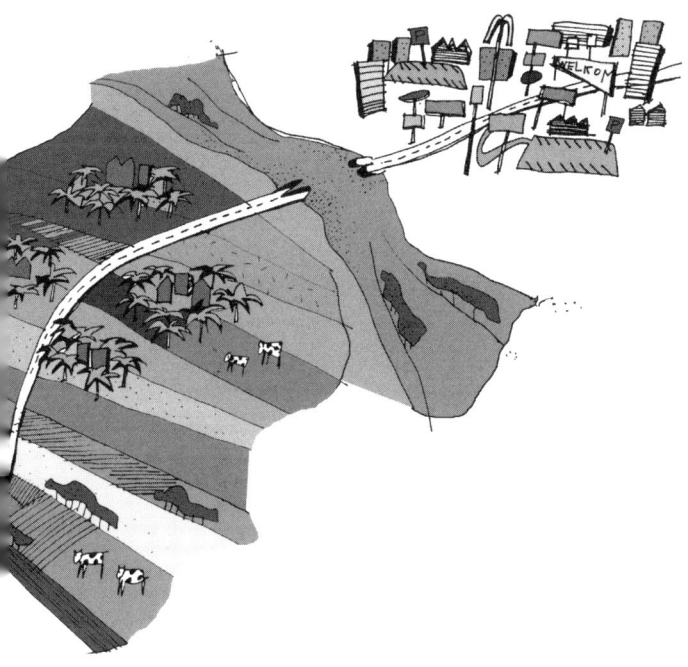

The motorway as design assignment
The Netherlands also has a rich tradition in the field of housing and urban planning: building houses, devising districts, planning complete towns. But there is no visionary tradition of urban planning for the design and development of the motorway. If you want to turn the motorway into a design assignment, two agreements have to be made.

The motorway must be given an aesthetic dimension, just like the streets of a city. Roads are there to transport commodities, people and ideas. If we move, whether by car, train or bicycle, we find ourselves in a different space. In designing places of this kind, we must adopt the perspective of the road user. A motorway is a public space too. We must develop a moving room with a view, and respect that point of view in our design practice.

Instruments are required to achieve an aesthetics of mobility, because existing urban planning practice is inadequate. An aesthetics of mobility is an aesthetics of the movement in which you are caught up at the points in time at which you are mobile. Through the alternation of different landscape and environmental elements, you can achieve an aesthetic effect like the cadence in a piece of music.

Six typologies
To give shape to the aesthetics of mobility, I introduce six typologies which can handle the alternation in the scale of the city and the scale of the landscape. Three of them are linked to the landscape: the panoramic landscape, the eco viaduct, and the Bali model. The other three are connected with the city: the Ruhr, Las Vegas, and La Défense. They form a series that extends from extremely rural to extremely urban.

From corridor to route

I make a proposal: the South corridor, which runs through Rotterdam from Antwerp to Paris, becomes the Erasmus route. The South-East corridor from Amsterdam to the southern Ruhr becomes the Rembrandt route; and the East corridor from The Hague to the northern Ruhr becomes the Couperus route. A thinker, a painter and a writer, each connected with culture and with one of the three main cities in the Netherlands.

I make an icon for each of the six typologies. You can compose and direct routes with it. The aesthetics of mobility acquires form. In this way you can respond to urban developments, design ecological main corridors, express changing landscapes, and direct economic developments. The selection of a specific type of economic activity can be regulated within one of the urban or rural typologies. You can arrange the space and indicate scale and size. The panoramic landscape in particular will have to be protected rapidly by laying down its dimensions.

Like a storybook

An even more attractive perspective is created if you turn a corridor into a story line. It is possible to give each route a character and identity of its own by linking it with themes, which may or may not be connected with the eponymous heroes of the routes. You can use the routes to show the beauty and strength of the Netherlands. They are the visiting cards of the Netherlands that handle large flows of people every day. Not only do we show the attractive, varied landscape with its wonderful works of art and water, but we also make it clear that there are beautiful cities in the Netherlands too. We show off the Netherlands as a main port and a brain port. You can also tell a historical story, as that is done along the Route du Soleil. Graphic designers can be brought in. But the landscape too, with its historical stratification, tells a story that has been neglected only too often until today. Historic points like the Hollandse Waterlinie – a strip of land flooded as a defence line – and the Stelling van Amsterdam defence system, as well as the Delta Works to keep out the sea, are splendid markers, and so are the various types of landscape. Where do you pass the ecological main structures, where are the badger tunnels? Which flora and fauna can you find here? It can all be visualised for the motorist. An aesthetics of mobility can become a sensorial experience that leads to knowledge.

---

223. Dutch infrastructure

224. The six typologies: from extremely rural to extremely urban

226. The routes are named

227. The aesthetics of mobility could become a sensory experience that leads to knowledge: defence line, badger tunnel, ecology, history, international port, water country
Not corridors but routes

228. Design of magnetic hovertrain through four types of landscape
Experience of town and country with the same speed of rail transport.
Below the experience of the same route accelerated in the rural areas and decelerated in the towns.

229. Design of construction of magnetic hover train

230. Zuyderzee route in North European fasttrack network: missing link
The rapid magnetic line leave the 'slow' landscape alone and offers opportunities for concentrated development at intersections

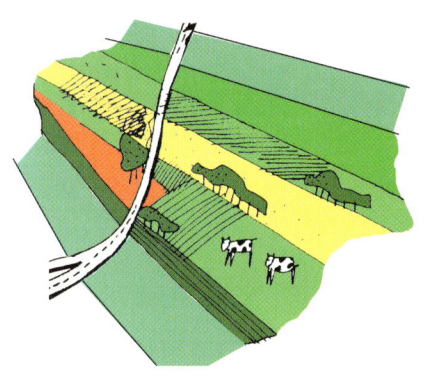 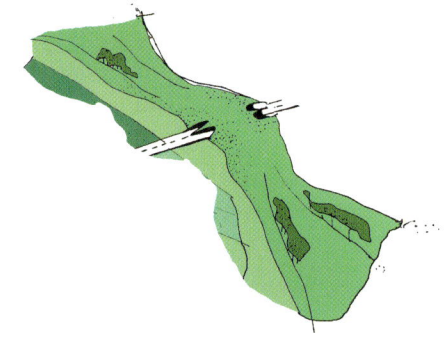 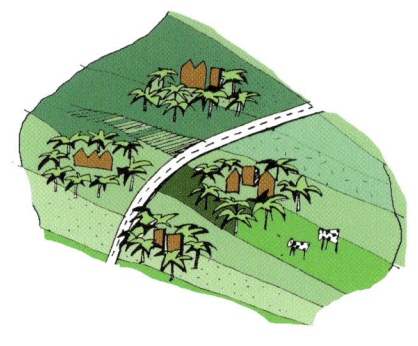

Panoramic landscape

This typology is an ode to the Dutch landscape: wide expanses, distant views, stage wings. The landscape of water, wind and clouds. This typology is about dimensions, about kilometres. It is not a foregone conclusion that it is about an unchanging situation that should be frozen or protected. That would not even be possible in the landscape whose essential characteristic is change. It is about the sensorial experience of the panoramic landscape as a typical Dutch identity.

Eco viaduct

This type is named after the eco viaducts, of which there are now three in the Netherlands. There should be more of them, and they should be much broader. They are places where we must allow the laws of nature to prevail over the infrastructure. Wide parks over the road correspond to this typology.

Bali model

The paradise-like landscape of Bali was in danger of being destroyed under the economic pressure to build hotels. To limit the damage to the landscape, it has been laid down that no buildings are to be higher than a palm tree. This stipulation is based on the idea that what you build must be in relation to the dimensions of the landscape. The principle of oases in the landscape also has a long history in the Netherlands. Just think of the villages on mounds in Friesland with their church towers soaring above the tops of the trees, or the farms in the flat countryside of Groningen surrounded by trees. The Bali typology can be used for small developments, which come to occupy the position of oases in the landscape. The principle is that no building should be taller than a tree.

  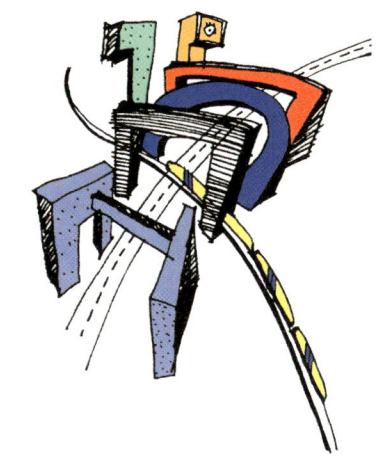

  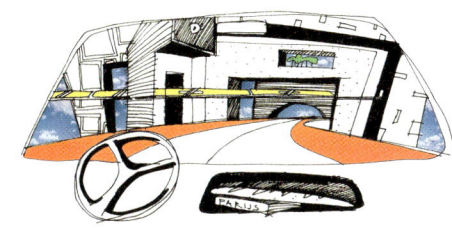

Ruhr

The Ruhr is the most urbanised part of Europe, but you do not realise that when you drive through it on the Autobahn. A strip of land has been reserved alongside the German motorways for possible further developments such as extra lanes, railway track or metro lines. That reserve space is planted with trees. It is as though you drive through large areas of woodland. The Ruhr typology could be used for new developments and especially to hide certain industrial sites from view.

Las Vegas

Las Vegas is the model for buildings intended to advertise that are orientated towards car drivers. Originally they were small or even tiny buildings with a huge advertising column in a gigantic car park. The built up area gradually grew denser and changed Las Vegas. The huge car parks were used as building land, the advertising columns disappeared, and the original buildings were replaced by huge ones that were themselves advertising objects. You can use the Las Vegas typology on locations where you eventually want to develop a high-quality, densely built up site that is clearly orientated towards the motorway. The design must take into account the time factor and the long-term ambition.

La Défense

It is characteristic of the La Défense type that infrastructure becomes a building. The most far-reaching case is that of La Défense in Paris, but in Barcelona too fantastic urban squares with pavilions have been built above motorways. On other locations the space beneath a raised motorway is used to build a large car park in combination with a rail station. You can see a step in this direction at the Utrechtse Baan in The Hague, but cities like Amsterdam, Utrecht and Maastricht also call for this approach. The link with high-quality regional and international public transport is a natural one.

From fragmentation to a wide basis of support

Motorways cross local authority, provincial and national borders. A motorway from The Hague to the border near the German Ruhr intersects some thirty local authorities and three provinces. At the same time at least five ministries have an interest and a say in the motorways. So an integrated approach to the design of motorway routes entails administrative problems. The organisation and procedure of the Ministry of Transport, Public Works and Water Management are not attuned to this either.

Routes in search of a commission

The Netherlands is faced with a number of important decisions in the field of town and country planning. Globalisation of the economy, mobility, urban renewal and the 'growing sense of being full' play a role. It is an opportunity to design a coherent structure of motorways and cities with landscape form-scenarios. The Dutch landscape is defined as the interweaving of nature and culture. The mobility routes will play an important role in that, which is why they require vision and direction. And, even more important, the placement of a commission. This calls for a political administration that assumes its responsibility and an architect who is enabled to develop an integrated vision. The various ministries, the cabinet as a whole, and the mayors and aldermen will have to make daring choices along the axes of mobility when they place commissions. On the basis of these choices, public works and architecture can combine to develop an aesthetics of mobility entirely in the tradition of the Netherlands as a work of art.

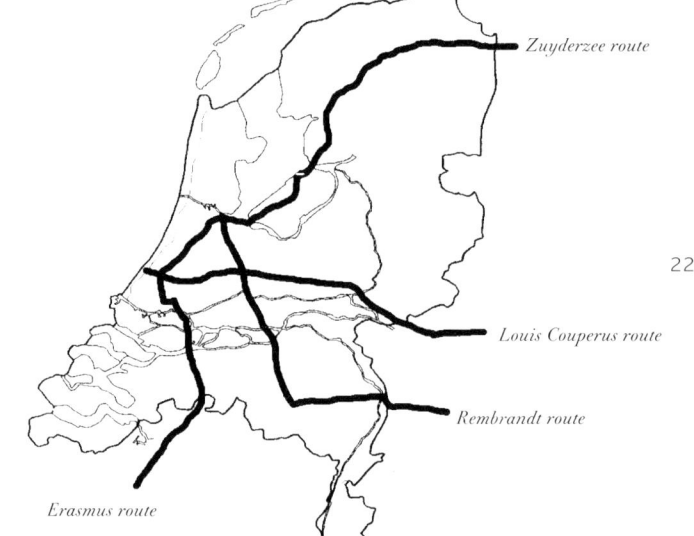

corridor route

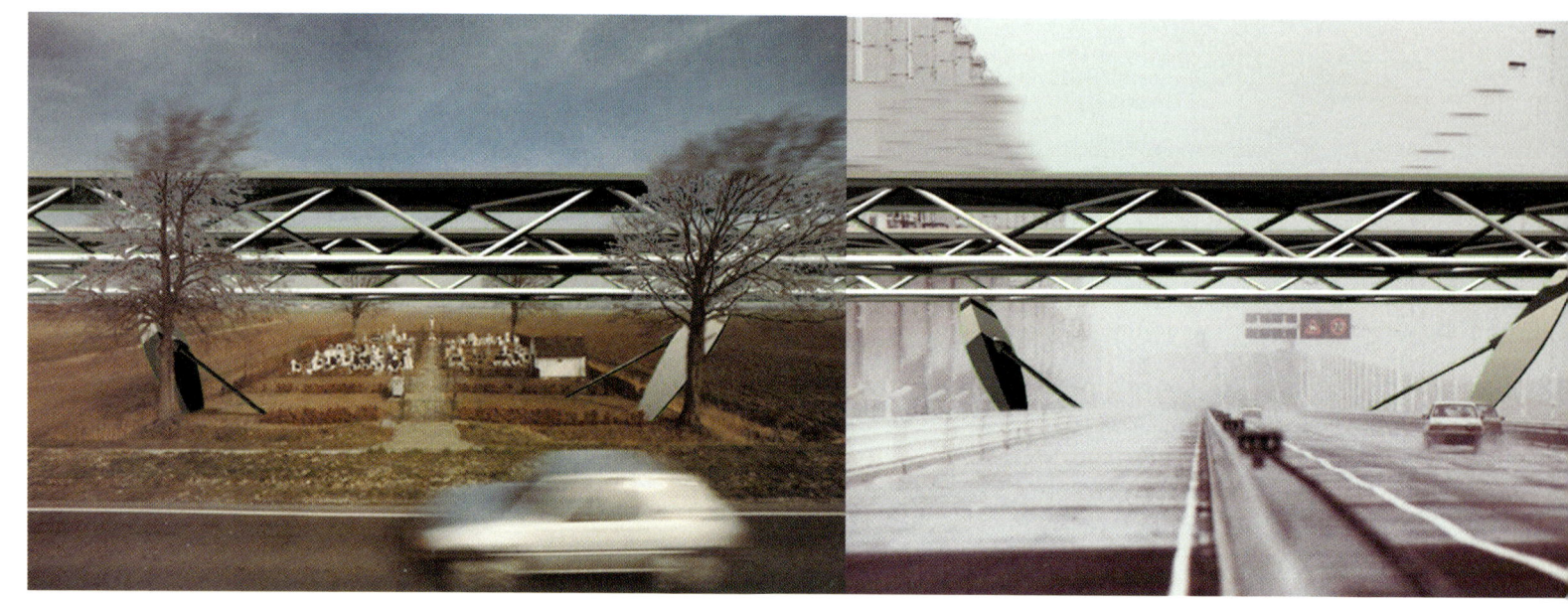

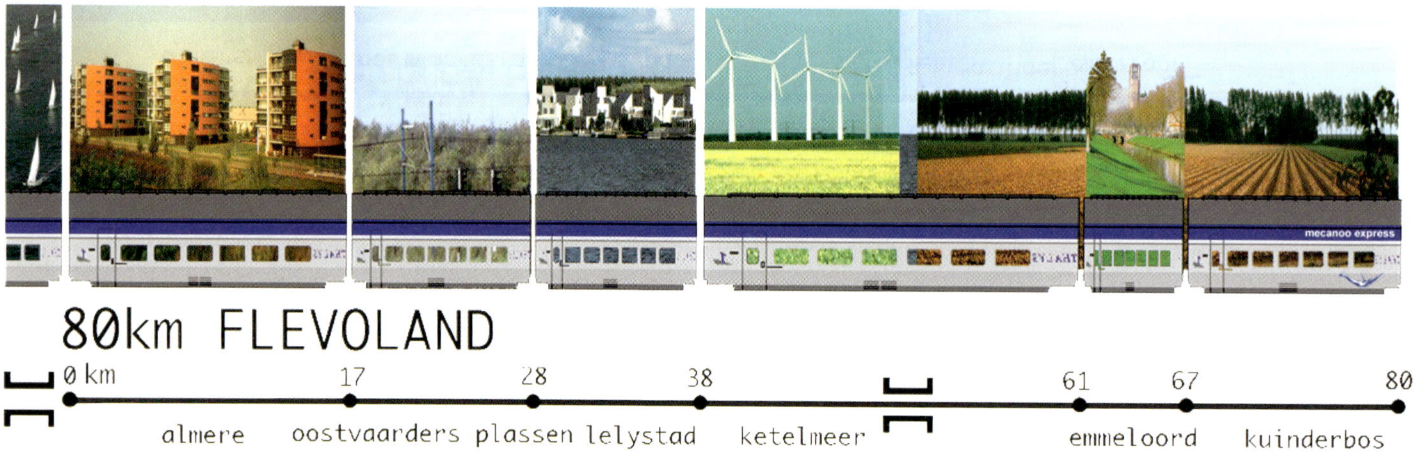
mecanoo express
80km FLEVOLAND
0 km
17
28
38
61
67
80
almere
oostvaarders plassen
lelystad
ketelmeer
emmeloord
kuinderbos

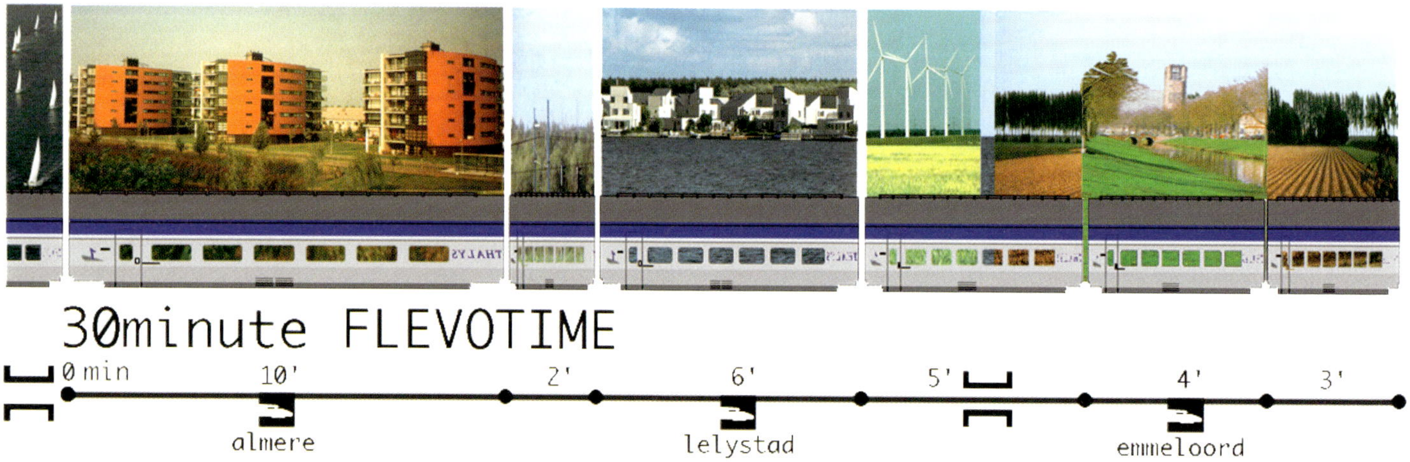
30minute FLEVOTIME
0 min
10'
2'
6'
5'
4'
3'
almere
lelystad
emmeloord

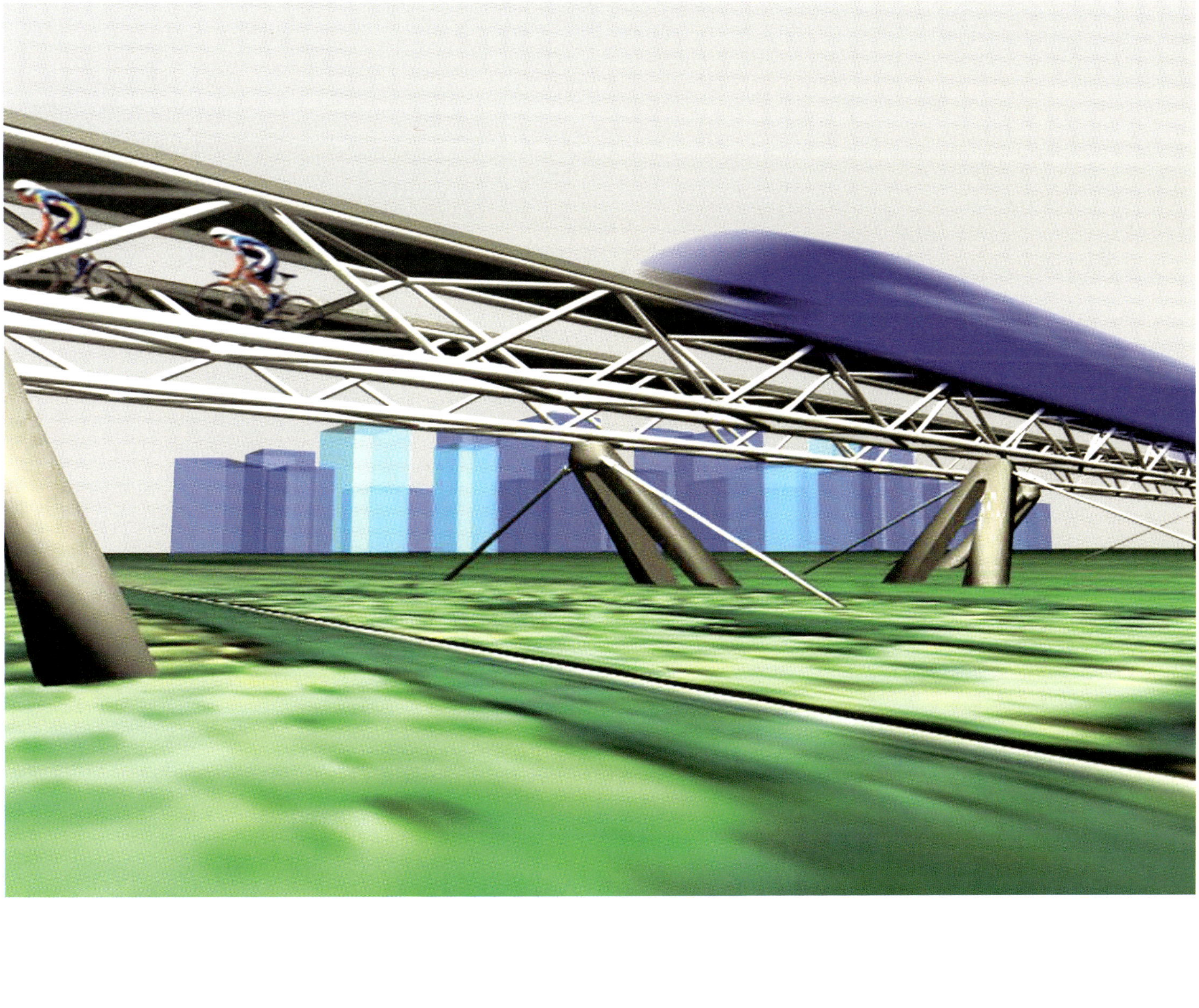

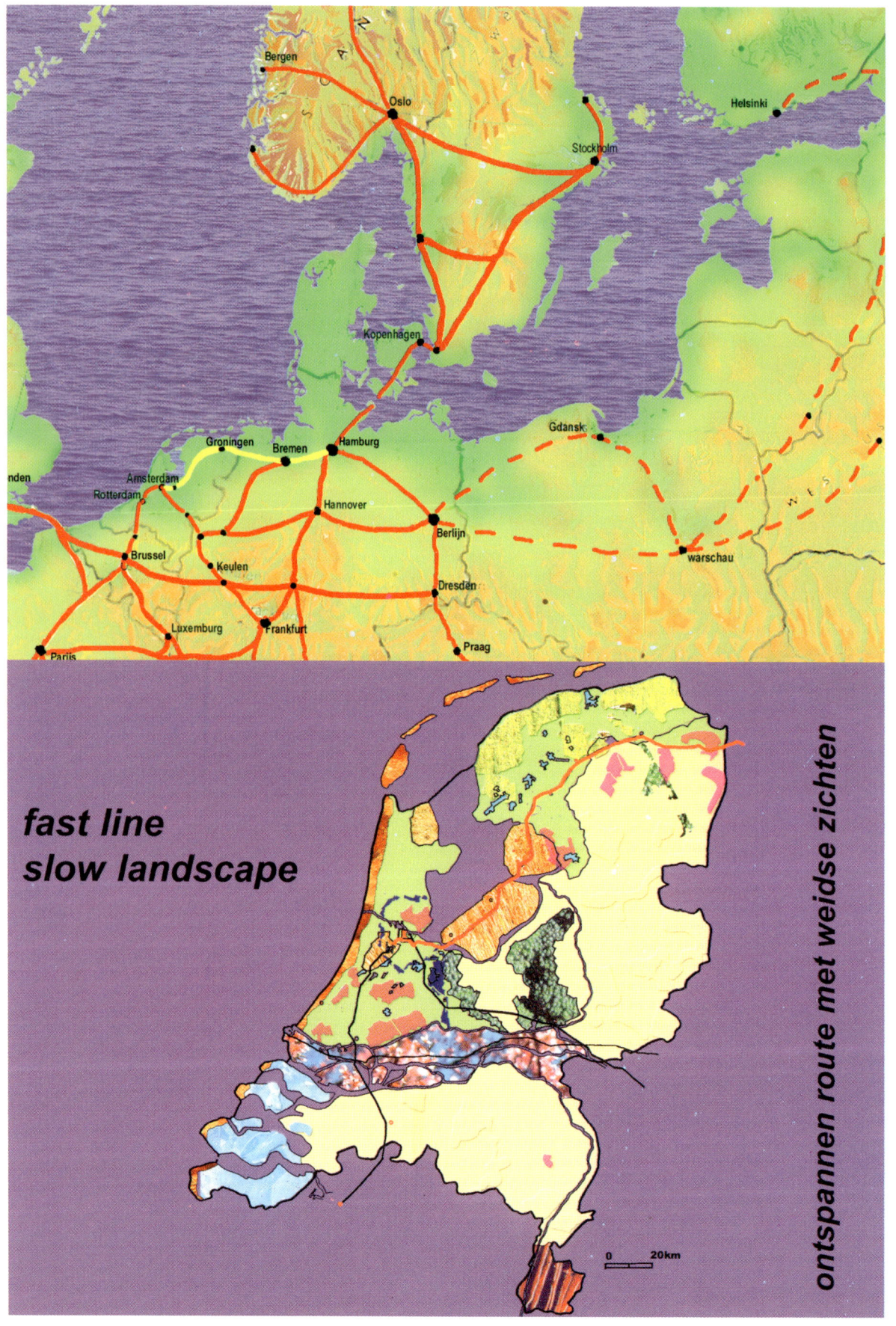

**fast line
slow landscape**

ontspannen route met weidse zichten

Postscript
The lecture on the need for an aesthetics of mobility that I give on 1 February 1999 for an audience invited by the Minister of Transport, Public Works and Water Management, Tineke Netelenbos, sparks off a number of reactions. It is published and frequently cited by professional journals and newspapers. The managers of the Netherlands then appear to take up the challenge and responsibility for placing commissions of large mobility axes. Eight local authorities join in asking for recommendations on a part of the Louis Couperus route. Four provinces ask for advice on the mobility axis from Amsterdam to Groningen. We call this fourth route through the Netherlands the Zuyderzee route: an ode to the history of the Dutch landscape, that is always subject to change. In the plan we study the implications of a fast magnetic hovertrain for a 'leisurely landscape' like that of Friesland and Groningen. We make drawings in which we show that the sense of fullness in the Netherlands is reinforced by the growth of mobility. The train (and the car) accelerate to maximum speed in the countryside, which reduces the time of the journey and also the duration of the experience of the countryside. The train slows down when it approaches a city, which prolongs the duration of the experience of the city. We make proposals for the construction of the hovertrain line and investigate it from the details of its construction to its embedding in the landscape.

The Zuyderzee route and the Louis Couperus route are two of the total of nine 'major projects' that are included in the Architecture Memorandum for the period 2000-2004. This memorandum is issued by four ministries – Education, Culture and Science; Housing, Spatial Planning and the Environment; Transport, Public Works and Water Management; and Agriculture, Nature Management and Fisheries – which indicates that the ministries are shouldering their joint responsibility. This unique cooperation between the ministries is a breakthrough in the practice of town and country planning.

That the universities are also taking the aesthetics of mobility seriously is shown by my appointment as Professor at the Università della Svizzera Italiana, Accademia di architectura in Mendrisio, Switzerland, and as Professor of Architectural Design at Delft Technical University with a new chair: the aesthetics of mobility.

Project specifications

Amsterdam canals
Canal house and L.A. Rieshuis, Amsterdam
Location: Brouwersgracht 280-282/Vinkenstraat 175-181
Design: 1995-1997
Execution: 1997-1998
Client: Woningbouwvereniging De Principaal v.o.f., Amsterdam
Design team: Francine Houben, Leen Kooman, Huib de Jong, Roelof Heida, Douglas Ardern, René Bouman
Structural engineer: Strackee Bouwadviesbureau b.v., Amsterdam
Contractor: Aannemersbedrijf J. Scheurer & Zn., Amsterdam

Twelve houses and a hotel
House and studio, Rotterdam
Design: 1989-1990
Execution: 1990-1991
Design team: Francine Houben, Erick van Egeraat, Theo Kupers, Bjarne Mastenbroek, Inma Fernandez-Puíg, Cock Peterse, Birgit Jürgenhake, Marjolijn Adriaansche
Structural engineer: ABT adviesbureau voor bouwtechniek b.v., Delft
General contractor: Van Omme & de Groot b.v., Rotterdam

Dancing blocks
Ringvaartplasbuurt Oost, Prinsenland
Location: Jacques Dutilhweg, Ariana Noorlandensingel, Geertrui Henningstraat, Neeltje Griffijnstraat, Klaas Dullemondstraat, Geertruida Breurstraat, Clazina Kouwenbergzoom, Rotterdam
Design: 1988-1991
Execution: 1991-1993
Client: Stichting Volkswoningen, Rotterdam
Design team: Francine Houben, Erick van Egeraat, Chris de Weijer, Dick van Gameren, Huib de Jong, Marjolijn Adriaansche, Sylvie Beugels, Cock Peterse
Structural engineer: Groenendijk en Poot, Rotterdam
General contractor: Volker Bouwmaatschappij, Rotterdam

Space for space
Reorganisation of public space, Groningen city centre
Location: Groningen city centre
Design: 1989-1990
Client: Groningen Local Authority, Town and Country Planning Department
Design team: Francine Houben, Erick van Egeraat, Pim Köther, Ton Salman, Theo Kupers, Leen Kooman, Marjolijn Adriaansche, Astrid Huwald, Bjarne Mastenbroek

Intimacy and reconciliation
Herdenkingsplein [Commemorative Square], Maastricht
Design: 1990-1992
Execution: 1993-1994
Client housing: Rabobank Pension Fund, Utrecht
Client square: Maastricht Local Authority
Design team: Francine Houben, Chris de Weijer, Erick van Egeraat, Nathalie de Vries, Huib de Jong, Marjolijn Adriaansche, Sylvie Beugels, Ard Buijsen, Kerstin Hahn, Birgit Jürgenhake, Theo Kupers, Toon de Wilde
Structural engineer: ABT adviesbureau voor bouwtechniek b.v., Delft
General contractor: Bouwmaatschappij Keulen b.v., Geleen

Kasbah in the polder
Faculty of Economics and Management, Utrecht University
Location: Padualaan 101, Utrecht
Design: 1991-1992
Execution: 1993-1995
Client: Stichting Financiering Exploitatie Huisvesting Uithof, Utrecht
Design team: Francine Houben, Chris de Weijer, Erick van Egeraat, Henk Döll, Aart Fransen, Monica Adams, Marjolijn Adriaansche, Carlo Bevers, Giuseppina Borri, Gerrit Bras, Birgit de Bruin, Ard Buijsen, Katja van Dalen, Annemieke Diekman, Harry Kurzhals, Miranda Nieboer, William Richards, Mechthild Stuhlmacher, Nathalie de Vries, Wim van Zijl, Henk Bouwer
Artists: Gera van der Leun, Henk Metselaar, Linda Verkaaik
Structural engineer: ABT adviesbureau voor bouwtechniek b.v., Delft/Velp
Management consultant: PRC Management Consultants b.v., Bodegraven
Mechanical and electrical engineering consultant: Technical Management b.v., Amersfoort
General contractor: Hollandsche Beton Maatschappij b.v., Utrecht
Gardening: Van Ginkel b.v., Veenendaal

School of the senses
Isala College, Silvolde
Location: Laan van Schuylenburg 8
Design: 1990-1993
Execution: 1993-1995
Client: Catholic Foundation for Secondary Education, Oude IJssel region
Design team: Francine Houben, Chris de Weijer, Erick van Egeraat, Sjaak Janssen, Maartje Lammers, Gert Wiebing, Toon de Wilde, Bernhard Verster, William Richards, Birgit de Bruin, Annemiek Diekman, Enrico Cerasi, Paddy Tomesen
Structural engineer: ABT adviesbureau voor bouwtechniek b.v., Delft/Velp
Mechanical and electrical engineering consultant: Ketel Raadgevende Ingenieurs, Delft
General contractor: Klaassen Bouwmaatschappij, Dinxperlo

Church and theatre
Trusttheater, Amsterdam
Location: Kloverniersburgwal 50
Design: 1995
Execution: 1996
Client: Trusttheater, Amsterdam
Design team: Francine Houben, Chris de Weijer, Michel Tombal, Francesco Veenstra, Ursula Fritz, Gerrit Schilder jr.
Project management: J. van Rijs, Amsterdam
Structural engineer: ABT adviesbureau voor bouwtechniek b.v., Delft/Velp
Mechanical engineering consultant: Ketel Raadgevende Ingenieurs, Delft
Building physics consultant: Peutz & Associés b.v., Mook
General contractor: Aannemingsmaatschappij Konst en Van Polen b.v., Westwoud

The ruin of beauty
Castle Ruins Cultural Centre, Deurne
Design: 1994
Client: Deurne Local Authority
Design team: Francine Houben, Theo Kupers, Daniëlle Huls

Library of the future
Library, Delft Technical University
Location: Prometheusplein 1
Design: 1993-1995
Execution: 1996-1998
Client: ING Vastgoed Ontwikkeling b.v., The Hague; TU Delft, Vastgoedbeheer, Delft
Design team: Francine Houben, Chris de Weijer, Aart Fransen, Carlo Bevers, Erick van Egeraat, Monica Adams, Marjolijn Adriaansche, Gerrit Bras, Ard Buijsen, Katja van Dalen, Annemiek Diekman, Alfa Hügelmann, Axel Koschany, Theo Kupers, Maartje Lammers, Paul Martin Lied, Bas Streppel, Astrid van Vliet, Henk Bouwer
Structural engineer: ABT adviesbureau voor bouwtechniek b.v., Delft/Velp
Mechanical engineering consultant: Ketel raadgevende ingenieurs b.v., Delft
Electrical engineering consultant: Deerns raadgevende ingenieurs b.v., Rijswijk
General contractor: Van Oorschot Versloot Bouw b.v.; Boele van Eesteren V.O.F. Rotterdam
Contractor façade: Scheldebouw architectural components, Middelburg
Gardening: Van Ginkel b.v., Veenendaal

Brasserie Blauw, redesign of the Aula, Technical University Delft
Location: Prometheusplein
Design: 1998
Execution: 1999
Client: TU Delft Vastgoedbeheer, Delft
Design team: Francine Houben, Alfa Hügelmann, Carlo Bevers, Maaike Bruins, Tom Grootscholten, Angelique Wisse, Henk Bouwer
General contractor: G.G. Kunz b.v., Delft
Project furniture and fittings: Van Gils Projecten b.v., Emmen

Changement
Westergasfabriek, Amsterdam
Location: Westergasfabriek site
Design: 1997
Client: Westerpark District Authority
Design team: Kathryn Gustafson in collaboration with Francine Houben, Joke Klumper, Ana Rocha

Master plan Westergasfabriek
Location: Westergasfabriek site
Design: 1998-1999
Client: Projectgroep Westergasfabriek, Amsterdam; MAB b.v., The Hague
Design team: Francine Houben, Joke Klumper, Ana Rocha, Francesco Veenstra,
Chris de Weijer, Robert Alewijnse, Judith Egberink, Cristina Fernandez

Buildings Westergasfabriek, Amsterdam
Location: Westergasfabriek site
Design: 2000
Execution: 2000-2002
Client: MAB b.v., The Hague
Design team: Francine Houben, Leen Kooman, Francesco Veenstra, Ana Rocha

Eco city, nature city, water city
Almere 2015
Design: 1995
Client: Almere Local Authority; B.V.R., Utrecht
Design team: Francine Houben, Iemke Bakker, Katja van Dalen, Robert Alewijnse,
Loes Oudenaarde, Annemiek Punter

Strategy of haste
Location: Almere suburbs
Design: 1997
Client: Almere Local Authority
Design team: Francine Houben, Iemke Bakker, Joke Klumper, Tom Berkhout

Gesture in the landscape
National Heritage Museum, Arnhem
Location: Schelmseweg 89
Design: 1995-1998
Execution: 1999-2000
Client: National Heritage Museum, Arnhem; Government Buildings Department,
Eastern Division, Arnhem
Design team: Francine Houben, Michel Tombal, Aart Fransen,
Chris de Weijer, Alfa Hügelmann, Joke Klumper, Pascal Tetteroo, Patrick Eichhorn,
Rick Splinter, Michael Dax, Saskia Hebert, Theo Kupers
Structural engineer: Goudstikker-de Vries/ACN b.v., Capelle a/d IJssel
Project management: ARBA MINCH projectmanagement B.V., The Hague
Mechanical and electrical engineering consultant: Technical Management, Amersfoort
General contractor: Strukton Bouwprojekten b.v., Maarssen

A house to work in
Maliebaan 16, Utrecht
Location: Maliebaan 16
Design: 1996-1999
Execution: 1998-2000
Client: Andersson Elffers Felix, Utrecht
Owner: J.H. Fentener van Vlissingen
Design team: Francine Houben, Francesco Veenstra, Berthe Jongejan, Ana Rocha,
Martin Stoop, Pascal Tetteroo, Henk Bouwer
Artist: Linda Verkaaik, Nijkerk
Structural engineer: ABT adviesbureau voor bouwtechniek b.v., Delft
Mechanical and electrical engineering consultant: Adviesbureau Hendriks b.v., Voorthuizen
Contractor: Aannemersbedrijf Van Zoelen b.v., Utrecht
Gardening: Van Ginkel Veenendaal b.v., Veenendaal

Triumph of Spirit over Matter
Opera Décor
Design: 1999
Execution: première 10 March 2000
Client: The Hollandia Dramatic Company
Design team: Francine Houben, Alfa Hügelmann, Anthony Hoete, Jasper Kaarsemaker

St Mary of the Angels
R.C. Chapel, Rotterdam
Location: Nieuwe Crooswijkseweg 123
Design: 1998-1999
Execution: 2000-2001
Client: St. Lawrence Cemetery, Rotterdam
Design team: Francine Houben, Francesco Veenstra, Ana Rocha, Huib de Jong, Martin Stoop,
Natascha Arala Chaves, Judith Egberink, Henk Bouwer
Structural engineer: ABT adviesbureau voor bouwtechniek b.v., Delft

Between the Rotte and the motorway
Nieuw Terbregge, Rotterdam
Location: Willy Lagermanstraat, Marie Baronstraat, Zus Braunstraat, Willy den Oudenstraat,
Piet van de Polsingel
Design: 1998
Execution: 1999-2001
Client: Proper Stok Woningen b.v., Rotterdam
Design team: Francine Houben, Iemke Bakker, Ana Rocha, Toon de Wilde,
Gert Jan Bestebreurtje, Sylvie Beugels, Huib de Jong, Berthe Jongejan, Erik Mesman,
Christian Quesada van Beresteijn, Sander Vijgen
Structural engineer: Adviesburo J.J. Datema b.v., Woudenberg
Project management: Proper Stok Woningen b.v., Rotterdam
Building physics consultant: WE Adviseurs, Gouda

Rhapsody in Blue
Parkhotel, Rotterdam
Location: Westersingel 70
Design: 1998-2000
Execution: 2001-2002
Client: Bilderberg Groep, Renkum
Design team: Francine Houben, Michel Tombal, Anthony Hoete, Carlo Bevers,
Ellen van der Wal, Allart Joffers, Geert-Jan van Damme, Celio Vrolijk, Steven van Kooten
Project management: Ingenieursbureau Stevens & Van Dijkck, Zoetermeer
Structural engineer: Ingenieursbureau Zonneveld b.v., Rotterdam
Mechanical engineer: J. van Toorenburg, The Hague

Mecanoo Blue
4th Bienal Internacional de Arquitetura, São Paulo, Brazil
Location: Palace of Industry, Parque do Ibirapuéra, São Paulo, Brazil
Design: 1999
Exhibition: 20 November 1999 - 25 January 2000
Design team: Francine Houben, Henk Döll, Alfa Hügelmann, Hanneke Hollander,
Jasper Kaarsemaker, Ana Rocha, Angelique Wisse
Curator: Max Risselada
Coordination and contacts Brazil: Paul Meurs
Models: Henk Bouwer, Catrien Overmeire, Berthe den Dolder & Marius Voet,
Robert Nottrot in collaboration with Annelie Kattenbach, Thijs de Ruiter, Babette Schumacher

A room with a view
Art of engineering and aesthetics of mobility
Design: 1998-1999
Client: Ministry of Transport, Public Works and Water Management
Design team: Francine Houben, Ana Rocha, Fréderique van Andel

Zuyderzee Line
Location: provinces Flevoland, Friesland, Groningen, Drenthe
Design: 1999-2000
Client: Province Flevoland; Executive Board North Netherlands Cooperation Association
(Friesland, Groningen, Drenthe)
Design team: Francine Houben, Berthe Jongejan, Magnus Weightman, Kristel
Aalbers, Anthony Hoete, Sjoukje van Heesch, Yolanda Boekhoudt

Magnetic hovertrain
Design: 2000
Client: Magnetic Hovertrain Consortium (Siemens Nederland N.V., Ballast Nedam,
ABN AMRO Bank, Hollandse Beton Groep)
Design Team: Francine Houben, Anthony Hoete, Maarten Happaerts

Biography Francine Houben

1955 Born in Sittard, The Netherlands
1974 St. Maartenscollege in Haren/Groningen, Atheneum B secondary education
1978 Student member Architecture Education Committee
1980 First prize Kruisplein youth housing project, Rotterdam
1981 Döll-Houben-Steenhuis Firm of Architects
1984 Technical University Delft, Department of Architecture (graduation prize)
1984 Mecanoo Firm of Architects
1985 Grant for study trip to Japan, Ministry of Welfare, Health and Cultural Affairs
1987 Rotterdam-Maaskant Award for Young Architects
1989 Mecanoo Firm of Architects
1989 Jury Europan 1 The Netherlands
1990 5x5 Working Committee
1990 Jury Prix de Rome architecture
1990-1992 Arts Council, Architectural Events and Publications Working Committee
1990 Guest lecturer Philadelphia University, Philadelphia, U.S.A.
1990-1996 Board Netherlands Architectural Institute, Rotterdam
1991 Jury Rietveld Award
1992 The William Lyon Sommerville visiting lectureship, University of Calgary, Canada
1992 Lecture Escuela Técnica Superior de Arquitectura, Madrid, Spain
1993 Lecture ETH Zürich, Switzerland
1993 Lecture Architekten Forum, Zürich, Switzerland
1993 'Modernism without Dogma', lecture Columbia University, New York, U.S.A.
1994-1996 Board of Fine Art, Design and Architecture Fund
1994 Guest lecturer Berlage Institute, Amsterdam
1994 'Symbol, Imagery and Place', lecture Ontario Association of Architects, Ottawa, Canada
1995 Grant for study trip to Los Angeles, U.S.A., Ministry of Welfare, Health and Cultural Affairs
1995 Rietveld Lecture 'Composition-Contrast-Complexity', Utrecht
1996 Jury Awards of Excellence, Canadian Architect, Toronto, Canada
1996 Guest lecturer Oxford University, U.K.
1997-2000 Housing, Spatial Planning and the Environment Council, The Hague
1997 Lecture University of Reggio, Italy
1997 Lecture Aarhus School of Architecture, Aarhus, Denmark
1997 Lecture National Association of Swedish Architects, Malmö, Sweden
1997 Wüstenrot Stiftung Lesung, Technical University Berlin, Germany
1998 Jury Archiprix
1998 Frauen Bauen Lesung, University of Stuttgart, Germany
1998 Jury E.O. Weijers Foundation
1998 Lecture Europan 5, Bilbao, Spain
1998 'Forma y Frontera', lecture Querétaro, Mexico
1998 'The most malleable country in the world', lecture National Dubo Day, Amsterdam
1999 'Art of engineering and aesthetics of mobility', lecture Nieuwe Kerk, The Hague
1999 Lecture University of Michigan, Ann Arbor, U.S.A.
1999 Lecture Ordini degli architetti della provincia di Como, Como, Italy
1999 Jury Europan 5 Germany
2000 Disciplinary Committee Habiforum Supervisory Board, Multiple Use of Space Expertise Network
2000 Lecture Museo Nacional de Belles Artes, Buenos Aires, Argentina
2000 Lecture Universidad Nacional de Córdoba, Argentina
2000 Lecture University of Washington, Seattle, U.S.A.
2000 Lecture University of Oregon, Portland, U.S.A.
2000 Jury Maaskant Award, Rotterdam
2000 Lecture RIAI, Cork, Ireland
2000 Professor Delft Technical University, chair of aesthetics of mobility
2000 Professor Università della Svizzera Italiana, Accademia di architectura, Mendrisio, Switzerland

Bibliography

Mecanoo books

Cusveller, S. (ed.), *Mecanoo, vijfentwintig werken*, Rotterdam 1987
Döll, H., Egeraat, E. van (ed.), *Woningbouw Kruisplein, Anders wonen in Rotterdam*, Delft 1985
Döll, H., Maas, C. (ed.), *Komposities voor stad en woning*, Groningen 1989
Hollander, H., S. van Wees (ed.) *Mecanoo Blue. Composition, Contrast, Complexity*, Rotterdam 1999
Houben, F., P. Vollaard, L. Waaijers, *Mecanoo architecten, Bibliotheek Technische Universiteit Delft*, Rotterdam 1998
Houben, F., 'Ingenieurskunst en mobiliteitsesthetiek', in: *Architectuur en de openbare ruimte, de dynamische delta 2*, The Hague 1999
Houben, F., *Maliebaan 16, een huis om in te werken*, Utrecht, Delft 2000
LeCuyer, A.W. (ed.), *Mecanoo*, Michigan 1999
Rood, L., N.T. Prat, *Mecanoo architekten*, Madrid 1994
Somer, K., *Mecanoo*, Rotterdam 1995

Selected television programmes

De kans om te bouwen, film by Rob Klaasman and Maarten Kloos, VPRO, 17 March 1985
De toekomst zal prachtig zijn, part 2, on Prinsenland, VPRO, 1992
FEM Future, Rondleiding Francine Houben, 11 October 1995
Het oude slot, zes visies op een beeldenpark, film by Maartje Seyfert and Victor Nieuwenhuis, September 1999
'Het woonhuis van architect Francine Houben' in: *TV Woonmagazine*, Veronica, 8 and 9 April 2000
I want to change the world, CNN, 1999
Jeugddromen, EO, 11 January 1997
Moois, Dag van de architectuur [Architecture Day], T.V. Rijnmond, 1 July 2000
Nachtgedachten, part 3, KRO, 26 September 1999
Nieuw Nederlands Peil, part 13, ID TV Amsterdam, 3 May 1998
Nu is verleden tijd, KRO, 25 November 2000
Panorama Vrijdag, on the Trusttheater, NPS, 1996
Roerend Goed, Architectuur van de sociale woningbouw, VPRO, 18 January 1994
TROS Nieuwshow, TROS, 26 June 1999
Voor en Tegen, Humanistische Omroep, 22 October 1999

Selected project publications

Canal house and L.A. Rieshuis, Amsterdam

Assche, P. van, 'Ergänzungsübungen, Wohnungsbau von Mecanoo und Claus & Kaan in Amsterdam', in: *Bauwelt*, no. 3, 15 January 1999, pp. 124-125
Berg, R. van den, 'Eerste homo-bejaardenhuis opent deuren.', in: *De Gay Krant*, no. 369, 9 October 1998, p. 13
'Brouwer III' and 'Vinkenstraat 175-179', in: *Projectdocumentatie woningbouwplannen Amsterdam 1996/1997*, Amsterdam 1997, pp. 64-65, 74
'Dutch Duet, Two housing schemes, Amsterdam, The Netherlands', in: *The Architectural Review*, November 1999, pp. 61-63
Ibelings, H. (ed.), 'Homobejaardenhuis', in: *Architectuur in Nederland. Jaarboek 1998-1999*, Rotterdam 1999, p. 33
Metz, T., 'Do the Dutch Do It Better?, An aging population poses new challenges to a nation known for humanely housing all', in: *Architectural Record*, no. 1, January 1998, pp. 122-123

House and studio, Rotterdam

'A house in Rotterdam, The Netherlands', in: *European Contemporary Houses*, 1998, pp. 47-51
'Architecten van deze eeuw, Mecanoo – Eigen Woonhuis, Rotterdam (1989-1991)', in: *Cobouw*, 14 April 1999
'Cañas y vidrio, Vivienda y estudio en Rotterdam', in: *Arquitectura Viva*, no. 31, July/August 1993, pp. 50-53
Confurius, G., 'Clair Obscur, Wohnhaus Mecanoo in Rotterdam', in: *Bauwelt*, vol. 83, no. 23, 12 June 1992, pp. 1266-1275
'Elegante Randerscheinung, Rotterdam', in: *Raum & Wohnen*, no. 1, 1993, pp. 32-35
'En verre et en bambous entre lac et canal', in: *Archicréé*, no. 249, September 1992, pp. 98-101
Koster, E., 'Modernisme als stijl, Woonhuis met studio van Mecanoo', in: *De Architect*, no. 4, 1992, pp. 104-111
'Maison-atelier à Rotterdam', in: *Architecture Aujourd'hui*, no. 286, 1993, pp. 26-31
'Mecanoo', in: *Building Design*, 24 April 1992, pp. 16-17
'Mecanoo', in: *Contemporary European Architects*, vol. II, pp. 126-133
'Mecanoo: Ein Hauch von Japan, Mecanoo: A touch of Japan', in: *Daidalos*, no. 54, 15 December 1994, pp. 30-33
'Mecanoo. House with studio. Kralingse Plaslaan, Rotterdam, The Netherlands', in: *GA Houses*, no. 40, 1994, pp. 45-57
'Mecanoo, Rotterdam 1989-1991', in: *Arquitecto*, pp. 110-117
'Modernistische rijkdom', in: *Stijl, norm en handschrift in de Nederlandse architectuur*, Rotterdam 1992, pp. 318-321
Oxenaar, A., 'Een nieuwe jas voor het modernisme', in: *Architectuur in Nederland. Jaarboek 1991/1992*, Rotterdam 1993, pp. 104-111
'Residence with studio in Rotterdam, Mecanoo Architekten b.v.', in: *Architectural Houses*, no. 2, 1997, pp. 116-129
'Schermi Sapienti, van Egeraat & Houben a Rotterdam: studio e abitazione', in: *Abitare*, no. 313, December 1992, pp. 36-40
'Wohnhaus mit Studio in Rotterdam', in: *Deubau-Kongress 1998*, 1998, pp. 150-151
Zalingen, M. van, 'Heel bewust gebouwd en toch vrij', in: *Eigen Huis & Interieur*, March 1995, pp. 70-77

Ringvaartplasbuurt Oost, Prinsenland, Rotterdam

Adriaansz, E., 'Mecanoo bouwt Tuinstad Prinsenland', in: *Het Financieele Dagblad*, 20 February 1993, p. 15
Grünhagen, H., 'Een groene buurt met een hoge dichtheid', in: *Woningraad Magazine*, no. 1, 1993, pp. 20-23
Huber, J., 'Die Architektengruppe Mecanoo in Holland', in: *Element*, no. 31, 1994, pp. 99-101
Koschany, A., 'Ein Siedlung tanzt aus der Reihe', in: *Das Bauzentrum*, no. 1, January 1994, pp. 18-25
Looise, W., 'De architect als koning in Prinsenland', in: *De Architect*, no. 41, 1990, pp. 40-45
Luca, G., 'Mecanoo Quartierre Prinsenland, Rotterdam', in: *Domus*, no. 745, January 1993, pp. 38-47
'Mecanoo', in: *Space Design*, February 1999, pp. 24-27
Oosterman, A., 'Prinsenland. Voorbeeldige architectuur van de jaren negentig', in: *Woningbouw in Nederland*, Rotterdam 1996, pp. 118-119
Primas, U., *Die Leere zwischen den Häusern*, no. 255, 2 November 1993, p. 11
'Prinsenland Wohnprojekt', in: *Debau-Kongress 1998*, 1998, pp. 154-156
Reijnddorp, A., 'El pais de los infante, hoe stedelijk is de nieuwe tuinwijk van Mecanoo', in: *De Architect*, vol. 24, June 1993, pp. 67-75
Stipa, A., 'Mecanoo, Cio che è realmente importante è unire alla forma l'emozione', in: *Controspazio*, no. 2, 1994, pp. 38-45
'Woonbuurt', in: *Architectuur in Nederland. Jaarboek 1993-1994*, Rotterdam 1994, pp. 69-74

Reorganisation of public space, Groningen city centre

Cusveller, S., 'Het vacuüm van de stad', in: *Locus Seminar*, no. 3, 1992, pp. 10-14
Harsema, H. (gen. ed.), Cusveller, S., Bijhouwer, R., 'Ruimte voor ruimte in de Groninger binnenstad', in: *Landschapsarchitectuur en stedebouw in Nederland 95-97*, Bussum 1998, pp. 146-149
'Het masterplan voor de stad Groningen', in: *Grafisch Nederland*, 1992, pp. 48-50
Kok, A., 'Niemand wist waar het heen zou gaan', in: *Binnenstad Beter*, May 1997, pp. 31-34
Mecanoo Architekten, *Ruimte voor Ruimte*, Groningen/Delft 1990

Herdenkingsplein [Commemorative Square], Maastricht

Brouwers, R. (ed.), 'Herdenkingsplein', in: *Architectuur in Nederland. Jaarboek 1994-1995*, Rotterdam 1995, pp. 124-127
'Épuré, 40 appartements à Maastricht, Pays-Bas', in: *Techniques & Architecture*, no. 425, April 1995, pp. 85-88
Genders, Ch., 'Actuele architectuur in Maastricht 1976-1996', in: *Bouwen als buitenkunst*, Maastricht 1996, pp. 57-58
'Herdenkingsplein in Maastricht, Niederlände', in: *Architektur + Wettbewerbe*, no. 161, March 1995, pp. 22-23
'Herdenkingsplein Maastricht, Mecanoo', in: *Lotus International*, no. 92, March 1997, pp. 56-58
'Herdenkingsplein, Mecanoo (Maastricht)', in: *Stylos Jaarboek 1994/95*, Delft 1995, p. 116-118
Lootsma, B., 'Abstecher nach Maastricht, Side Trip to Maastricht', in: *Daidalos*, no. 60, June 1996, pp. 92-93
'Maastricht Historic Quarter Apartments', in: *The Architecture of Multiresidential Buildings*, New York 1997, pp. 76-83
'Maßstabswechsel, Wohnungen am Herdenkingsplein in Maastricht', in: *Bauwelt*, vol. 86, no. 18, 1995, pp. 1040-1043

'Mecanoo, 40 Apartments in Maastricht, Netherlands', in: *Arquitectura Viva*, no. 53, November 1995, pp. 88-91
Oosterman, A., 'Herdenkingsplein', in: *Voorbeeldige architectuur van de jaren negentig*, Rotterdam 1996, pp. 116-117
'Rezidenza su una piazza a Maastricht, Olanda', in: *Housing*, no. 7/8, October 1997, pp. 60-61
Romijn, C., 'Architecten en hun favoriete bouwwerk', in: *Limburgs Dagblad*, 4 September 1999, p. 42
Stamm-Teske, W., *Preiswerter Wohnungsbau in den Niederlanden 1993-1998*, Düsseldorf 1998, pp. 108-111
Stieber, N., 'Modern Departures', in: *Progressive Architecture*, June 1995, pp. 96-101
'Wohnanlage "Herdenkingsplein" in Maastricht, Niederlände', in: *Architektur + Wettbewerbe*, no. 167, September 1996, pp. 8-9

Faculty of Economics and Management, Utrecht

Cleef, C. van, 'Kasbah Quads', in: *The Architectural Review*, no. 1192, June 1996, pp. 63-67
Coppola Pignatelli, P., in: *L'architettura della università*, Rome 1997, pp. 140-144
'Facolta di studi economici e management', in: *L'industria italiana del cemento*, July/August 1999, pp. 560-573
'Faculteitsgebouw', in: *Architectuur in Nederland. Jaarboek 1995-1996*, Rotterdam 1996, pp. 62-67
'Faculty of Economics and Management', in: *International Architecture Yearbook*, no. 3, 1997, pp. 80-81
'Faculty of Economics and Management, Utrecht Polytechnic University, The Netherlands', in: *5th Mies van de Rohe Pavilion Award for European Architecture*, Milan 1997, pp. 112-115
'Faculty of Economics', in: *The Architecture of Glass: Shaping Light*, Barcelona 1997, pp. 20-31
'Fakultät für Wirtschaftswissenschaften und Management', in: *Deubau-Kongress 1998*, 1998, pp. 152-153
Hofmaan, H., 'Informell, Fakultät für Wirtschaftswissenschaften und Management Utrecht College', in: *AIT, Architektur Innenarchitektur Technischer Ausbau*, no. 5, May 1996, pp. 41-45
Houben, F., 'Die Innenhoffe der Wirtschaftsfakultät in Utrecht', in: *Topos*, no. 12, September 1995, pp. 70-76
Huisman, J., 'Moeder der kunsten bedreigd', in: *de Volkskrant*, 29 June 1996, p. 43
Imagawa, N., 'Faculty of Economics and Management, Utrecht Polytechnic', in: *Space Design*, no. 389, February 1997, p. 21
'Kashba van Mecanoo', in: *Items*, vol. 14, no. 7, 1995, p. 12
Labree, A., 'Een Kabshba in de polder', in: *Glas in beeld*, vol. 8, no. 1, February 1997, pp. 6-11
Lootsma, B., 'Mecanoo, Facoltà di economia aziendale, Faculty of economics and management, Utrecht', in: *Domus*, no. 785, September 1996, pp. 16-23
Maas, T., '"Gevoelige architectuur" buitenkans toeleveranciers', in: *Cobouw*, no. 16, 26 January 1999, p. 7
'Mecanoo, Faculty of Economics and Management, Utrecht Polytechnic, The Netherlands 1991-1995', in: *Architecture and Urbanism*, no. 312, September 1996, pp. 20-35
Meens, N., 'Auf dem Campus von Utrecht, Ein Masterplan und drei Neubauten für den Uithof', in: *Bauwelt*, no. 43/44, 21 November 1997, pp. 2470-2471
Mos, P. de, 'Hogeschool – Architectuur, Mecanoo', in: *OntwerpDossier*, no. 1, Doetinchem, March 1997
Roos, R., 'Architectuur bij nacht. De twinkeling van een stedelijke kroonluchter', in: *BladNA*, no. 1, January 1998, pp. 8-9
Roos, R., 'Zwevende dozen', in: *Trouw*, 27 May 1995, p. 23
Rooy, M. van, 'Grenzeloze Ontwerpzucht. In de Utrechtse universiteitswijk de Uithof dansen de gebouwen', in: *NRC Handelsblad*, 1 November 1997, p. 53
Somer, K., 'Wirtschaftfakultät in Utrecht', in: *Baumeister*, vol. 93, no. 11, November 1996, pp. 34-39
Tummers, Nic. H.M., 'Rietveldprijs 1997, Bouwen aan de stad Utrecht 1995-'96', in: *Rietveldprijs 1997*, Bussum 1997, pp. 6-7, 16
'Un claustro abierto, Facultad de Económicas y Empresariales, Utrecht', in: *Arquitectura Viva*, no. 53, March/April 1997, pp. 90-97
Voorthuijsen, A. van, 'Zoveel ruimte in een glazen doos', in: *Utrechts Nieuwsblad*, 9 October 1999, p. 51
'Wirtschaftsfakultät der Universität Utrecht, Niederlände', in: *Architectur + Wettbewerbe*, June 2000, pp. 26-29

Isala College, Silvolde

Groenhart, L., 'Silvolde: Karaktervolle nieuwbouw Isala College', in: *Stedenbouw*, vol. 45, no. 516, 1994, p. 15-16
Hulsman, B., 'Renaissance in scholenbouw ondanks geldgebrek', in: *NRC Handelsblad*, 29 September 1999, p. 11
'Isala College', in: *International Architecture Yearbook*, no. 3, 1997, p. 87
'Isala College Silvolde', in: *Zodiac*, no. 18, pp. 170-173
Mecanoo, 'Inspiratie uit Oude IJssel en jong publiek', in: *Bouwdetail*, vol. 1, no. 2, March 1997, p. 40-45
'Middelbare School', in: *Architectuur in Nederland. Jaarboek 1995-1996*, Rotterdam 1996, pp. 56-61
'Nederland naar school. Twee eeuwen bouwen voor een veranderend onderwijs', in: *De Architectuurkrant*, no. 20, December, January, February 1996-1997
Rodermond, J., 'Vreemd en toch zo vertrouwd, Isala College in Silvolde van Mecanoo', in: *De Architect*, vol. 26, October 1995, pp. 78-83
Veenendaal, A., 'Scholenbouwprijs 1996', in: *Schooldomein*, vol. 9, no. 3, January 1997, pp. 31-34
Werner, F.R., 'Floating objects', in: *Bauwelt*, no. 14, April 1995, pp. 780-785

Trusttheater, Amsterdam

Agricola, E., 'Trusttheater in voormalige Lutherse Kerk', in: *Zichtlijnen*, no. 49, November 1996, pp. 4-8
Assche, P. van, 'Theater De Trust in Amsterdam', in: *A+Architctuur*, no. 5, October/November 1997, p. 41
Davey, Peter (ed.), 'Theatrical flair, An eighteenth-century Amsterdam church has been imaginatively transformed (if temporarily) into a theatre', in: *The Architectural Review*, no. 6, June 1999, pp. 86-89
Deuss, B., 'Ontwerpers van huizen met een ziel, Nederlandse theaterarchitecten in Praag', in: *Zichtlijnen*, no. 65, June 1999, p. 24
'Eerste theaterontwerp van Mecanoo, De Trust neemt bescheiden intrek in godshuis', in: *Projekt & Interieur*, vol. 8, no. 2, April 1997, pp. 42-44
Gompes, L., 'Het filosofisch geweld van De Trust', in: *Uitkrant*, December, 1996, p. 7
Jagt, M. van der, 'In Nieuw Trust-theater is van geldnood een deugd gemaakt', in: *de Volkskrant*, 20 December 1996, p. 13
Janssen, H., 'Slijmfiguren tussen aanrecht en wasmand, Het is lekker warm, de stoelen zitten goed', in: *de Volkskrant*, 23 December 1996, p. 9
'Nieuw Trusttheater geopend', in: *NRC Handelsblad*, 23 December 1996, p. 7
Rooy, M. van, 'Beladen speelgrond, Trusttheater op de Kloverniersburgwal', in: *Trust toneel*, no. 5, August 1996
Schwebel, H., 'Von der Kirche zur City-Kirche?, Umbau und Nutzung historischer Kirchengebäude', in: *Bauwelt*, no. 8, 21 February 1997, pp. 353-359

Somers, M., 'Vertrouwde Schwab in gloednieuw eigen theater', in: *Het Parool*, 17 December 1996
'Trust-Theater, Amsterdam', in: *Deubau-Kongress 1998*, 1998, p. 158
Uhde, R., 'Homopathischer Eingriff, Umwandlung einer ehemaligen Kirche zum Theater', in: *Bausubstanz*, January 2000, pp. 14-17
'Umnutzung in den Niederlanden', in: *Umnutzungen im Bestand neue zwecke für alte Gebäude*, 2000, pp. 72-77
'Van kerk tot archief tot Theater', in: *Cobouw*, no. 242, 24 December 1996, p. 3

Castle Ruins Cultural Centre, Deurne

Meurs, P., 'Nieuw: Re-Arch.', in: *De Architect*, no. 10, October 1995, pp. 24-25
Provoost, M. (ed.), 'Kasteel Deurne', in: *RE-ARCH nieuwe ontwerpen voor oude gebouwen*, Rotterdam 1995, pp. 106-113

Library, Delft Technical University

Assche, P. van, 'Frog Needs Grass, Universitätsbibliothek in Delft', in: *Bauwelt*, vol. 89, no. 9, April 1998, pp. 752-757
'Aufbruch, Mecanoo bauen eine High-Tech-Bibliothek mit Abluftfassade auf Delft's Uni-Campus', in: *AIT, Architektur Innenarchitektur Technischer Ausbau*, no. 8, Spezialausgabe Intelligente Architektur, March 1997, p. 16
Betsky, A., 'Through the roof, In Delft, Mecanoo builds a library for the digital age', in: *Architecture*, October 1998, pp. 124-133
'Bibliotheek TU Delft, Library, Delft University of Technology', in: *Architectuur in Nederland. Jaarboek 1997/1998*, Rotterdam 1998, pp. 130-135
Bouwens, C., 'Delft, Bibliotheek Technische Universiteit', in: *Duurzaam Bouwen*, no. 2, March 1998, pp. 40-43
'Bücher am Bahnhof', in: *Neue Zürcher Zeitung*, 23 August 1999, pp. 25-26
'Dutch Divergence, Comment', in: *The Architectural Review*, March 1999, p. 35
Englert, K., 'Grass über die Moderne wachsen lassen, Ein intimes Bücherdrama: Die neue Universitätsbibliothek von Delft', in: *Frankfurter Allgemeine Zeitung*, no. 270, 20 November 1998, p. 43
Ganapati Raman, P., 'I confini di una practica riflessiva, The limits of a reflective practice', in: *Spazio e società*, January/March 2000, pp. 62-75
'Grandes nomes da arquitetura holandesa do pos-guerra...', in: *Projeto Design*, no. 239, January 2000, pp. 80-81
Haan, H. de, 'Een bibliotheek als een enorme luchthavenhal', in: *de Volkskrant*, 30 December 1997, pp. 14
Hoete, A., 'The Hillding, From the recent crop of Dutch public architecture emerges a curious building', in: *Monument*, no. 31, August/September 1999
Jap Sam, E., 'Grass, glass and cyberspace', in: *Frame*, May/June 1999, pp. 42-47
Koster, E., 'Bibliotheek als sculptuur, architectonische vrijheid in het tijdperk van de electronische snelweg', in: *Het Financieele Dagblad*, 21 and 23 February 1998, p. 29
Krijgsman, H.G., 'Toppunt van leesplezier, Centrale Bibliotheek TU Delft', in: *Bouwen met Staal*, November/December 1997, p. 30-37
Krol, J., 'Intensieve interactie tussen architect en betrokken en staat centraal', in: *Bibliotheekblad*, no. 12, 16 June 2000, pp. 18-19
Lootsma, B., 'University library, Delft, The Netherlands', in: *Domus*, no. 812, February 1999, pp. 22-29

'Mecanoo architecten, Bibliotheek Technische Universiteit, Delft', in: *Zodiac*, no. 18, September 1997, pp. 162-173
'Mecanoo architekten, Library of the Delft University of Technology', in: *GA Document*, no. 55, June 1999, pp. 90-103
Melet, E., 'Zoeken naar het Afschuwwekkende Schone', in: *De Architect*, no. 60, October 1995, pp. 16-25
Prack, F., 'Mecanoo holandeses e innovadores', in: *Arquitectura*, no. 316, 19 April 2000, pp. 4-5
Rodermond, J., 'Hybride Architectuur, Bibliotheek van Mecanoo in Delft', in: *De Architect*, no. 2, February 1998, pp. 50-61
Schweighüfer, K., 'Delfter Spitze', in: *Häuser*, no. 3, 1999, pp. 48-52
Seron-Pierre, C., 'La cinquième façade, Delft, Pays-Bas, Bibliothèque universitaire', in: *AMC Le Moniteur Architecture*, no. 102, November 1999, pp. 84-85
'Teknik Üniversite Kütüphanesi, Delft, Hollanda', in: *Mimarlik*, November 1999, pp. 51-54
'Vegetatiedak op driehoog achter', in: *Groen*, no. 9, September 1998, pp. 8-9
Vollaard, P., 'Een driehoek van glas en gras', in: *Architectuur & Bouwen*, vol. 12, no. 2, February 1997, pp. 30-33
Vries, T. de, 'Intellectueel ruimteschip veilig geland', in: *Architectuur & Bouwen*, no. 10, October 1998, pp. 34-39
Weiss, K.D., 'Bücher hinter Glas und Gras, Organisations des Wissens: Die neue Bücherei der Universität Delft setzt Maßstabe im Bibliotheksbau', in: *Berliner Zeitung*, 20 November 1998, p. 13
Weiss, K.D., 'Zauberberg der Wissenschaften, Hochschulebibliothek der TU Delft, Niederlände', in: *Architektur Aktuell*, no. 223, December 1998, pp. 50-63, 118
Wöhler, T., 'Lichtes Lernen, Bibliothek Technische Universität Delft/NL', in: *Deutsche Bauzeitschrift*, no. 11, November 1999, pp. 52-57
Wortmann, A., 'De louteringsberg van Mecanoo, Universiteitsbibliotheek in Delft', in: *Archis*, no. 3, March 1998, pp. 66-73

Westergasfabriek, Amsterdam

Andela, G., 'Westergasfabriek Amsterdam, Vijf Parkontwerpen', in: *Archis*, no. 9, September 1997, pp. 14-21
Duijvelshoff, K., 'Westerpark, De visie van Kathryn Gustafson in samenwerking met Francine Houben op het toekomstige park', in: *Nieuwsbrief*, Westerpark City District, September 1997
'Frans ontwerp voor Westerpark, Fonteinen in park moeten geluid weren', in: *Het Parool*, 2 July 1997
Klein, A., 'The grounds of the Westergasfabriek', in: *The park of the future*, no. 1, 1997, pp. 5-9
Kruyver, M., 'Geen stenen maar gras/Not stones but grass', in: *The park of the future*, no. 2, April 1998, pp. 18-21
Leeuwen, R. van, 'Vijf plannen voor het Westerpark', in: *Groen*, no. 11, November 1997, pp. 8-17
Lookman, W.M., 'Bodemsanering geeft mede vorm aan stadspark', in: *Het Financieele Dagblad*, 2 December 1998, p. 2
Piët, S. en Evert Verhagen, 'Changement, Plan Kathryn Gustafson/Mecanoo Architekten', in: *Een park voor de 21ste eeuw*, Bussum 1998, pp. 52-61
Sierksma, P., 'Westerpark met station ontsluiten', in: *Trouw*, 26 June 1997, p. 21
Snoeijen, M., 'Amsterdam verkoopt cultuurmonumenten aan projectontwikkelaar, Overheid niet in staat tot renovatie', in: *NRC Handelsblad*, 22 November 1999
'Terrein voormalige gasfabriek wordt Amsterdams stadspark', in: *Het Financieele Dagblad*, 26 June 1997
Verhagen, E., 'Masterplan van Francine Houben', in: *Stad en groen*, Town and Country Planning Department, Amsterdam City Council, no. 3, September 1999, pp. 14-17
Vermeulen, J., 'En de winnaar is...', in: *Staatscourant*, July 1997

Vermeulen, J., 'Onthechting op fabrieksterrein', in:
NRC Handelsblad, 4 July 1997
Vugts, P., 'Westergasfabriek krijgt stukje winstpotentie', in:
Het Parool, 8 October 1999, p. 7
'Westerpark/Terrein Westergasfabriek (P)', in:
Gids voor de Nederlandse Tuin- en landschapsarchitectuur,
Rotterdam 1998, pp. 137-138

Almere 2015

Cusveller, S., 'Almere tast de horizon af, op zoek naar haar
toekomst', in: *Blauwe Kamer*, no. 2, April 1997, pp. 22-30
Houben, F., 'Almere, city in the "Gooi" region', in:
Urban Design International, no. 1, March 1997, pp. 13-21
Houben, F., I. Bakker, K. van Dalen, A. Punter, 'Mecanoo,
Almere 2005-2015', in: *Lotus International*, no. 96,
March 1998, pp. 84-85
Lont, Y., *Bijlagen bij de ruimtelijke ontwikkelingsstrategie
Almere 2015*, BVR adviseurs stedelijke ontwikkeling
en management bv, pp. 73-106
Lont, Y., *Ruimtelijke ontwikkelingsstrategie Almere 2015*,
BVR adviseurs stedelijke ontwikkeling en management bv
Maven, A., 'Tre progetti del gruppo Mecanoo', in:
Paesaggio Krbano, no. 6, October/November 1998
Tilman, H., 'Almere na 2005', in: *De Architect*, vol. 28, no. 3,
March 1997, pp. 19-21

National Heritage Museum, Arnhem

Dirks, B., 'Een openluchtmuseum is meer dan nostalgie
alleen', in: *de Volkskrant*, 11 April 1998, p. 3
Futugawa, Y., 'Mecanoo. Dutch Open-air museum, Arnhem,
The Netherlands', in: *GA Document*, no. 58, April 1999,
pp. 59-63
Groot, H. de, 'Landschap met bol en streep', in: *Het Houtblad*,
no. 4, June 2000, pp. 32-37
Houben, F., 'Die muur is de trots van de Nederlandse bouw',
in: *Cobouw*, 19 May 2000
Houben, F., 'Een gebouw als een gebaar in het bos', in:
Nederlands Openluchtmuseum, 2000, pp. 6-11
Huisman, J., 'De muur en de kei', in: *Vrij Nederland*, 20 May 2000
Hulsman, B., 'Humorvolle nieuwbouw van Openluchtmuseum',
in: *NRC Handelsblad*, 31 May 2000
Ibelings, H., 'Een poëtische staalkaart van baksteen', in:
de Volkskrant, 26 May 2000
'Jan Vaessen: markante, eigenwijze cultuurheld', in: *Bouw*,
no. 6, June 2000, pp. 13-14
Melet, E., 'Zoeken naar het afschuwwekkende Schone', in:
De Architect, October 1995, pp. 16-25
Nauta, H., 'Vogelvlucht door Nederlandse geschiedenis
in koperen ei', in: *Trouw*, 26 May 2000
Rodermond, J., 'Beweging in het landschap', in:
De Architect, July/August 2000, pp. 42-47
Rodermond, J., 'Heterogeen, maar gelijksoortig.
De onopgemerkte doorbraak van het postmodernisme', in:
De Architect, January 1999, p. 31
Schmidt, M., 'Het ei en de muur als concept', in:
Het Parool, 29 May 1996, p. 13
Slessor, C., 'Figures in a landscape', in: *The Architectural
Review*, no. 8, August 2000, pp. 61-65
Stungo, N., 'Ova take', in: *Ribajournal*, June 2000, pp. 8-9
Vries, T. de, 'Mecanoo werpt koperen (k)ei', in:
Detail in Architectuur, no. 5, May 2000, pp. 20-25

Wind, H., 'Koperen kei', in:
Bouwwereld, no. 5, 6 March 2000, pp. 16-19
Winkler, O., 'Eingangsgebäude und HollandRama des
Freilichtmuseums in Arnheim', in: *Baumeister*, no. 8, August
2000, pp. 40-45

Maliebaan 16, Utrecht

'Dubbel grondgebruik', *Cobouw*, 20 June 2000, p. 2
Havik, K., 'Transformatie van villa tot villa, Uitbreiding
en renovatie kantoor A.E.F. in Utrecht van Mecanoo', in:
De Architect, September 2000, pp. 50-55
Houben, F., *Maliebaan 16, een huis om in te werken*,
Utrecht/Delft 2000
Voorthuijzen, A. van, 'Mecanoo ondergronds op Maliebaan',
in: *Utrechts Nieuwsblad*, 1 July 2000
'Werken onder de wortels. Monumentale stadsvilla Utrecht
verrijkt met ondergrondse uitbreiding', in: *Projekt & Interieur*,
no. 5, October 2000, pp. 70-73

Opera décor Triumph of Spirit over Matter

Cerny, M., 'Genietbare opera van Hendrickx', in:
Het Nieuwsblad/De Goutenaar, 13 March 2000
Friche, M., 'Double lyrique pour petits et grands', in:
Le Soir, 13 March 2000
'Houben maakt operadecor', in:
Detail in Architectuur, no. 6, June 2000, p. 7
Lint, P. van der, 'Tussen de stoelen van Rietveld', in:
Trouw, 14 March 2000, pp. 60-75
Moens, S., 'Gezocht: een sterkere componist
en een veel sterkere librettist', in: *De Morgen*, 13 March 2000

R.C. Chapel, Rotterdam

Houben, F., 'Een kapel voor de Rooms-Katholieke
Begraafplaats Crooswijk', in: *Architectuur Agenda*, Rotterdam,
September 1999
Hulsman, R., 'Rooms-Katholieke Begraafplaats Crooswijk', in:
Stedenbouw van de dood, Rotterdam, September 1999

Nieuw Terbregge, Rotterdam

Boer, H. de, 'Water-, land- en singelpracht. Vinex-locatie
Nieuw-Terbregge Rotterdam', in: *Het Houtblad*, no. 5,
September 2000, pp. 4-9
'De Landjes', in: *Plan Nieuw Terbregge te Rotterdam –
Hillegersberg*, Rotterdam 2000
'Duurzaam en energiezuinig bouwen a/d Rotte', in:
Stedebouw & Architectuur, no. 1, February 1999, pp. 4-5
Moscoviter, H., 'De dubbele straat als oplossing', in:
Rotterdams Dagblad, 12 July 2000
'Waterwoningen', in: *Plan Nieuw Terbregge te Rotterdam –
Hillegersberg*, Rotterdam 2000

4th Bienal Internacional de Arquitetura, São Paulo, Brazil

'4ª Bienal International de Arquitetura', in: *Folha de São Paulo*, 20 November 1999
'Aire libre para Mecanoo Bleu', in: *El Cronista*, 26 April 2000
Glusberg, J., 'Bienal de arquitetura apunta al gran publico', in: *Ambitio Financiero*, 30 November 1999
Hollander, H., Sander van Wees (ed.), *Mecanoo Blue. Composition, Contrast, Complexity*, Rotterdam 1999
'Mecanoo: architecture of poetry', in: *Buenos Aires Herald*, 26 April 2000, p. 17
'Mecanoo blue', in: *AIT, Architektur Innenarchitektur Technischer Ausbau*, no. 3, March 2000, p. 9
'"Mecanoo bleu" naar Argentinië', in: *Delftsche Post*, 15 March 2000
'Mecanoo holandeses e innovadores', in: *La Nación*, no. 316, 19 April 2000, pp. 4-5
'Mecanoo op tournee', in: *De Architect*, no. 4, April 2000
Meyer, M., 'Modernism without dogma', in: *Buenos Aires Herald Magazine*, May 2000, pp. 24-25
'Nederlandse architectuur naar São Paulo. Drieluik "Het modernisme voorbij" op architectuurbiënnale in Brazilië', in: *Apeldoornsche Courant*, 19 October 1999
'Nederlandse architectuur op biënnale São Paulo', in: *Rotterdams Dagblad*, 16 October 1999
'O olhar do outro', in: *Arquitetura & Urbanisme*, no. 88, February/March 2000, pp. 64-65
Prack, F., 'Mecanoo holandeses e innovadores', in: *La Nación*, no. 316, 19 April 2000, pp. 4-5
'Prijzen voor de Nederlandse presentatie op de Internationale', in: *B-nieuws*, no. 16, 10 April 2000, pp. 6-9
'Prijzen voor Nederlandse presentatie', in: *De Bouwadviseur*, 1 June 2000
'Reflexion en Accion', in: *Arquitetura*, 3 May 2000
'Reflexión en acción', in: *El Cronista*, 3 May 2000, pp. 6-12
Rocha, R., 'Uma cidade melhor', in: *Problemas Brasileiros*, March/April 2000, p. 27
Roes, E., 'Nederlandse Architectuur in Brazilië', in: *De Telegraaf*, 22 October 1999
Simoes, A., 'Sintese para o próximo seculo', in: *Lux journal, Gazeta Mercantil São Paulo*, 26 November 1999, p. 14
'Werk Mecanoo op internationale beurs', in: *Delftsche Courant*, 15 March 2000

The art of engineering and the aesthetics of mobility

Boer, J., 'Beleef de snelweg', in: *Carp*, no. 16, 18 April 2000, pp. 32-33
Haaft, G. ten, 'Een scherm kent geen seizoenen', in: *Trouw*, 10 December 1999
Houben, F., 'Aesthetics of Mobility', in: *Monument*, December 1999, pp. 40-41
Houben, F., 'De esthetiek van de snelweg', in: *Blauwe Kamer*, no. 6, December 1999, pp. 22-23
Houben, F., 'Ingenieurskunst en mobiliteitsesthetiek, de dynamische delta', in: *Architectuur en de openbare ruimte, De dynamische delta 2*, The Hague 1999, pp. 20-39
Houben, F., 'Ingenieurskunst en mobiliteitsesthetiek', in: *Stedebouw & Ruimtelijke ordening*, vol. 80, no. 3, 1999
Houben, F., 'Mecanoo, mobiliteitsesthetiek versus corridorvorming', in: *Architectuur in Nederland. Jaarboek 1999-2000*, Rotterdam 2000, pp. 9-12
Ibelings, H., 'Bali langs de A27', in: *de Volkskrant*, 6 August 1999
Maas, T., 'We moeten nog leren corridors te ontwerpen', in: *Cobouw*, no. 24, 5 February 1999, p. 9
Voorthuijsen, A. van, 'De blikvangers langs de snelweg.', in: *Veluws Dagblad*, 30 October 1999, p. 59

Selected Awards

1987
Rotterdam-Maaskant Prize for Young Architects, for whole oeuvre

1990
Nieuwe Maas Prize for urban renewal, Hillekop, Rotterdam

1993
Berlage Flag for Gravura Lithographers, The Hague

1994
Jhr. Victor de Stuers Medal for Herdenkingsplein [Commemorative Square], Maastricht

1996
First prize for the best school building 1996 for Isala College, Silvolde
Nomination Mies van der Rohe Pavilion Award for European Architecture 1996 for Faculty of Economics and Management, Utrecht University

1998
National Steel Prize for the Library of Delft Technical University

2000
4th Bienal Internacional de Arquitetura Award for the exhibition 'Mecanoo Blue – *Composition, Contrast, Complexity*, Fundaçao Bienal de São Paulo, Brazil
Corus Construction Award for the Millennium, for the Library of Delft Technical University
Rotterdam Bouwkwaliteitsprijs 2000, for housing Nieuw Terbregge, Rotterdam
First prize TECU Architecture Award 2000 for the Dutch National Heritage Museum, Arnhem

Selected exhibitions

1985
'Biënnale Jonge Architecten 1985', Beurs van Berlage, Amsterdam (The Netherlands)

1985-1989
'l'Architecture est un jeu magnifique', travelling exhibition opening at Centre Pompidou, Paris (France)

1987
Seaside landscape for the New Netherlands,
'Nieuw Nederland' exhibition, Beurs van Berlage, Amsterdam (The Netherlands)

1988
'Reweaving the Urban Fabric; International Approaches to Infill Housing', Thomas Paine Gallery, New York (USA)

1989
'La Biennal de Barcelona, Young Architects in Europe', Barcelona (Spain)

1992
Retrospective 'Obra Reciente', Colegio Oficial de Arquitectos de Madrid, Madrid (Spain)

1993
'Mecanoo: ein junges Architektenteam aus Delft', Architektur Forum, Zürich (Switzerland)
'Een nieuwe impuls voor de tuinwijk, de tuinen van Prinsenland', Netherlands Architectural Institute, Rotterdam (The Netherlands)

1994
'Prinsenland', Dutch Embassy, Lima (Peru)

1995
'design NOW! design from the Netherlands', Centre de design de l'Université du Québec à Montréal (Canada)

1996
'National Identity. Aspects of European Design', Louisiana Museum of Modern Art, Humlebaek (Denmark)
'Arquitectos Sin Fronteras'. 19th international UIA congress, Colegio Oficial de Aparejadores y Arquitectos Técnicos de Barcelona, Barcelona (Spain)

1998
'Ve Prix européen d'architecture. "Pavillon Mies van der Rohe"', Paris (France)

1999
'Mecanoo, the reflective architect', travelling exhibition opening at the College of Architecture + Urban Planning, University of Michigan, Ann Arbor (USA)
'GA International', GA Gallery, Tokyo (Japan)
'Mecanoo. Nederlands Openluchtmuseum – een verhalende muur met een mystieke zwerfkei.',
Netherlands Architecture Institute, Rotterdam (The Netherlands)
'Mecanoo architecten. 1:20 – 1:200 – 1:200.000. Stoel, Schuur, Streek.', ABC Architectural Centre, Haarlem (The Netherlands)
'Mecanoo. Opere e progretti.', Pinacoteca Civica, Como (Italy)
'Mecanoo Blue - *Composition, Contrast, Complexity*.'
4th Bienal Internacional de Arquitetura, São Paulo (Brazil)

2000
'Mecanoo Blue - *Composition, Contrast, Complexity*.'
Museo Nacional de Belles Artes, Buenos Aires (Argentina)
'Mecanoo Poetics', Apeldoorn (The Netherlands)

2001
'*Compositie, Contrast, Complexiteit*', Netherlands Architecture Institute, Rotterdam (The Netherlands)

Mecanoo 2001

Francine Houben
Henk Döll

Michel Tombal
Aart Fransen
Leen Kooman
Iemke Bakker
Sylvie Beugels
Sjaak Jansen
Annelies van Eenennaam

Patrick Arends
Oscar Benet Ramos
Carlo Bevers
Henk Bouwer
Barbara van Boxtel
Sylvie Bruyninckx
Anne Busker
Peter Claeys
Nilvia Coffy
Sven Cordsen
Leon Delhez
Patrick Eichhorn
Markus Freigang
Michael Gore
Anthony Hoete
Hanneke Hollander
Thomas Huacuja-Gallmann
Alfa Hügelmann
Allart Joffers
Huib de Jong
Berthe Jongejan
Jasper Kaarsemaker
Marcel Kellner
Andrea Klerks
Joke Klumper
Jan Kooi
Olga Korstanje
Chris Luth
Jeroen Luykx
Judith Mastenbroek
Diana Meinster
Paul Meurs
Sylvia de Nolf
Simon Nuñez Arenas Fraile
Karoline Poorter
Kolja Preuss
Sjoerd Redel
Ana Rocha
Ellen Schindler
Ulf Schrader
Rick Splinter
Friso van der Steen
Martin Stoop
Pascal Tetteroo
Jason Torres
Francesco Veenstra
Sebas Veldhuisen
Bas Vijn
Uda Visser
Astrid van Vliet
Ellen van der Wal
Vanessa Wegner
Magnus Weightman
Bianca Wennekes
Toon de Wilde

This publication was made possible through the financial support of the Netherlands Architecture Fund.

Concept and text: Francine Houben
Photography: Christian Richters
Drawings: Mecanoo

Copy Editing:
Hanneke Hollander, Caroline Gautier, Paulina Damen

English translation:
Peter Mason

Image editing:
Francine Houben, Hanneke Hollander, Rick Splinter, Ellen Schindler

Graphic design:
Via Vermeulen/Rick Vermeulen, Gérard Konings

Other photographs and illustrations:
Aeroview Rotterdam (207); Ernest Annyas (139 bottom right and middle left); Michel Claus (119-122); Maarten Corbijn (back cover); The Eames Office (26); Editorial Gustavo Gili S.A., Barcelona 1996, 'Oscar Niemeyer' (212, 213); Flying Camera Eindhoven Airport (16); Gemeentearchief, Amsterdam (138); Rob 't Hart (215, 217 bottom); David Hockney Studio installation, Los Angeles, 1995, photo: Richard Schmidt (24); Francine Houben (8 top, 10, 48, 63, 71 top, 76 bottom left, 82, 95 bottom, 107 bottom); Marcel van Kerckhoven (57 bottom); KLM (135); Nelson Kon (216, 217 top, 218); Maarten Laupman (28 top); Jannes Linders (104, 167, 168 bottom); Patricia MacDonald (14 top); Meetkundige Dienst Rijkswaterstaat, Delft (15, 223 bottom right); Jaap Oosterhoff, Rietveld Schröder Archief (34); Peter de Ruig (73); Scagliola/Brakkee (50, 59, 60, 143, 144); Siebe Swart (139 top and middle right); Pieter Vandermeer (187, 190); Ger van der Vlugt (30); VWS (223 bottom left); Baron Wolman (14 b)

Production:
Caroline Gautier, Barbera van Kooij

Lithography and printing:
Die Keure, Bruges

A CIP catalogue record for this book is available from the Library of Congress, Washington D.C., USA.

Deutsche Bibliothek Cataloging-in-Publication Data

Francine Houben/Mecanoo architects : composition - contrast - complexity.
[Engl. transl.: Peter Mason]. - Basel ; Boston ; Berlin : Birkhäuser, 2001
ISBN 3-7643-6452-1

For works of visual artists affiliated with a CISAC-organization the copyrights have been settled with Beeldrecht in Amsterdam. © 2000, c/o Beeldrecht Amsterdam

It was not possible to find all the copyright holders of the illustrations used. Interested parties are requested to contact NAi Publishers, Mauritsweg 23, 3012 JR Rotterdam, The Netherlands.

This work is subject to copyright. All rights are reserved, whether the whole or part of the material is concerned, specifically the rights of translation, reprinting, re-use of illustrations, recitation, broadcasting, reproduction on microfilms or in other ways, and storage in data bases.
For any kind of use permission of the copyright owner must be obtained.

© Original Dutch edition: Francine Houben and NAi Publishers Rotterdam 2001

© 2001 Francine Houben and Birkhäuser – Publishers for Architecture
P.O. Box 133, CH-4010 Basel, Switzerland.
Member of the BertelsmannSpringer Publishing Group.
Printed on acid-free paper produced of chlorine-free pulp. TCF ∞
Printed and bound in Belgium
ISBN 3-7643-6452-1

9 8 7 6 5 4 3 2 1